Sewing LINGERIE *that* FITS

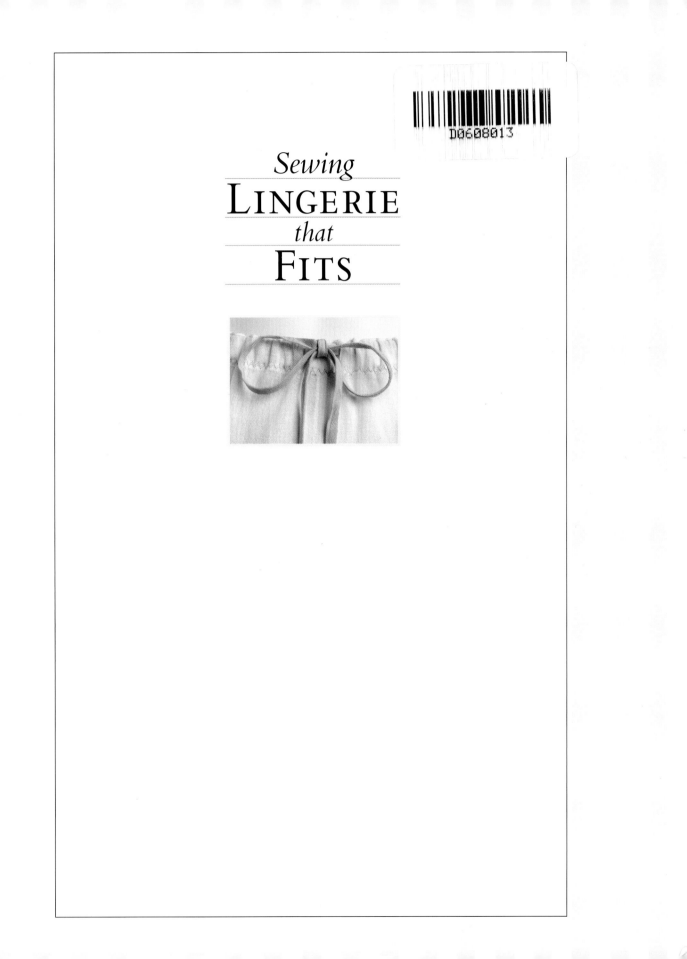

Sewing
LINGERIE
that
FITS

Stylish Underwear,
Sleepwear, and Loungewear for
Everyday Living

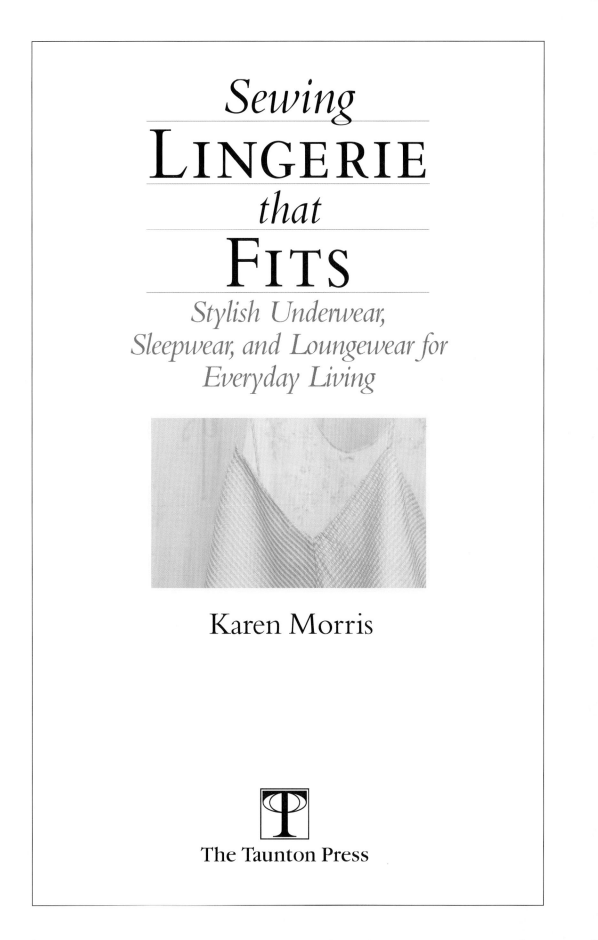

Karen Morris

The Taunton Press

Publisher: *Jim Childs*

Acquisitions Editor: *Jolynn Gower*

Editorial Assistant: *Meredith DeSousa*

Copy Editor: *Diane Sinitsky*

Indexer: *Lynda Stannard*

Cover and Interior Designer: *Gloria Melfi*

Layout Artist: *Catherine Cassidy*

Photographer: *Jack Deutsch*

Illustrator: *Christine Erikson*

Cover photo: Background gowns by designer Andra Gabrielle;
camisole by Karen Morris

Taunton
BOOKS & VIDEOS
for fellow enthusiasts

Printed in the United States of America
10 9 8 7 6 5 4 3 2 1

The Taunton Press, Inc.
63 South Main Street, PO Box 5506, Newtown, CT 06470-5506
e-mail: tp@taunton.com

Distributed by Publishers Group West

Library of Congress Cataloging-in-Publication Data
Morris, Karen.
Sewing lingerie that fits : stylish underwear, sleepwear, and
loungewear for everyday living / Karen Morris.
p. cm.
Includes index.
ISBN 1-56158-309-X
1. Lingerie. 2. Sleepwear. 3. Sewing. I. Title
TT670.M66   2001
646.4'204—dc21   00-051027

To my dear children Hannah and Sam, who
usually knew the answer when they asked, "Why
can't I use your computer to go on the Internet?"

ACKNOWLEDGMENTS

Besides all the wonderful folks at The Taunton Press,
especially Chris Timmons and Jolynn Gower,
I appreciate the contributions of the following people,
who taught me a lot about fine sewing and developed some
of the methods I used in this book:
Betty Auchard for information on leaf printing with
Inkodye (see *Threads* No. 47, pp. 62 to 65).
Jan Bones for the patternmaking instructions in chapter 4.
Cindy Elam of Élan Patterns for the wealth of bra information
in chapter 5 (see *Threads* No. 71, pp. 36 to 40)
and for the acid-dyeing information in chapter 6.
Andra Gabrielle, whose work redefined the word "fragile" for me
with her inspirational silk lingerie and sewing techniques
shown in chapter 6 and throughout this book
(see *Threads* No. 66, p. 96 and No. 68, pp. 28–33).
Joanne Molesky for the information on contrast binding
with elastic (see *Threads* No. 77, pp. 64–70).
Marcy Tilton for bias information (see *Threads* No. 76, pp. 34–39).
These back issues of *Threads* magazine were still available
when this book went to press. To order a back issue,
call (800) 888-8286.

CONTENTS

(Background garment by Andra Gabrielle.)

INTRODUCTION

Garment by Andra Gabrielle.

EVERYBODY WEARS lingerie. This broad category includes the first clothes we put on everyday and the last things we wear at night. These are probably the hardest-working and most frequently washed and worn garments in our entire wardrobes. And what we wear matters. We know just what we like and what we don't, and we're willing to try on, dig, and search to find just the right garments.

So why is it that more avid sewers don't create their own lingerie? Is it because we don't care so much about these garments that most others can't see? I don't think so. Women spend a lot of money buying beautiful lingerie, and I've always sensed that most women sew primarily for their own pleasure and satisfaction. We sew because we love to sew, we adore beautiful fabrics, and we enjoy wearing something that took shape in our hands. We also love to solve problems in our wardrobes. So it's a mystery to me why the majority of both serious and casual sewers don't make their own lingerie.

I think the problem is a lack of information about how to sew the garments they really want: comfortable, beautiful, long-lasting lingerie that fits. In the past, most lingerie information for home sewers has focused on inexpensive garments made of tricot and nylon lace. But if you can buy the same garment for $1.99, why bother sewing it? In this book, I encourage sewers to approach a whole new level of quality with the goal of creating beautiful and functional lingerie in the colors and fabrics they want, in their perfect sizes.

Perhaps some women don't sew lingerie because they think it's too difficult. The truth is just the opposite—nearly all lingerie garments are quick and easy to make. Also, many who aren't completely confident about their sewing abilities can rest easy: Nobody will be examining your buttonholes or checking to see how neatly you've finished every inside edge. You can wear and enjoy your very first attempt while you continue to refine and perfect the garment shape and your technique.

In fact, sewing your own lingerie gives you the freedom to work out the shape and fit you like, whether it's a structured bra or a simple panty that hits your waist at just the right spot. And the best part is that you can make it over and over again as you need more of that item in your wardrobe. Using your favorite fabrics and colors, you have the freedom to create absolutely anything you want—wild prints; soft, luxurious fabrics; a neon-orange panty with bright blue trim; or whatever makes you feel wonderful. Construction will become faster and easier every time, and you can tweak the style until you achieve that satisfying ideal—the perfect garment.

Besides these compelling reasons to sew lingerie, add the fact that women as consumers are basically at the mercy of lingerie manufacturers. Lingerie is one area where women need to find reliable styles that they can count on and continue to purchase year after year. But the reality is that lingerie is just another fashion industry; when you find a style you love, it has a good chance of being discontinued the next time you try to buy it.

If you're petite or taller than average, I'm sure you've found that slips, gowns, and sleeves tend to be the wrong length. And if you're plus-sized, hard-to-fit, or just not one of the "standard fashion sizes" stocked by lingerie departments, you'll probably end up choosing between beige, beige, and beige (if, that is, you can find anything that fits). I've read that 85 percent of women wear the wrong size bra; we're offered little guidance in selecting a size. Also, unless you're spending lots of money on designer lingerie, fabrics tend to be inexpensive synthetics, not so comfortable, and quick to wear out. So take charge of the situation, and sew your own. Your favorite bra or panty style will never be discontinued again!

If you still need a reason to get motivated, spend an hour browsing the lingerie department of the best store in your area to see what the high-quality lingerie designers and manufacturers are producing, lines such as Calvin Klein, Ralph Lauren, Hanro, Calida, and Natori. Notice the diversity of garments available, the fashion trends, and the high prices many of these pieces command (like $16 to $20 for panties, or a $49 crushed-velour camisole that would be easy to make in an hour using ½ yd. of $15-per-yd. stretch velour). Before you leave, try on a few of the most appealing garments and make notes about what you do and don't like, specific notes about fabric, style, shape, and fit. Then you'll be ready and motivated to go home and start sewing.

Once home, review your wardrobe of favorite lingerie, make a shopping list of patterns, fabrics, and findings you'll need, and begin to create your own perfect lingerie. Give yourself a break from sewing finicky, serious garments and make some quick, beautiful lingerie. Whether you answer the challenge of making the perfect bra for your body or just run up a few cushy loungewear pieces in superior fabrics and unique colors, you'll find that this type of sewing offers unexpected satisfaction and a large return for your investment of time and money. You'll never go back to "settling" for the limited choices you can scrounge up in stores.

(Background garment by Andra Gabrielle.)

WHAT IS LINGERIE?

The clothing category loosely called lingerie is simply huge. From bras and panties to yoga togs and polished loungewear, it keeps growing and expanding as our current wardrobe needs change and develop. The garment styles and shapes that make up the group known as lingerie are actually a wide and diverse collection of clothing in both traditional, predictable styles and modern, unexpected shapes.

Lingerie has always been a very personal matter. Especially today, women are able to choose between a variety of style options designed to accomplish the same purpose. So with all the choices in mind as you prepare to create your own lingerie, don't limit yourself to what catalogs of popular culture define as lingerie. While traditional styles may meet many of your needs, there are no hard and fast rules. Whatever you feel most comfortable wearing is what does the job best.

Lingerie As I See It

My definition of lingerie, as used throughout this book, is a broad one. It includes any garment that is worn as a first layer beneath other clothing (often called underwear, but I prefer the name innerwear); any garment worn for sleeping (sleepwear); and all the garments worn in relative privacy that are not intended to be seen by the general public, a category I call loungewear.

Most ready-to-wear lingerie is constructed from soft, comfortable knits, like this trio of practical, everyday innerwear.

Innerwear

The traditional innerwear group includes bras, camisoles, one-piece bodysuits and teddies, panties and tap pants, and half- and full-slips. Short and long johns, another type of innerwear, are a more seasonal option and are generally made of light, sleek knit fabrics from silk or fine wool to synthetics. They add warmth without bulk under day clothes and are available in a variety of styles, from a warm camisole and extended-leg briefs (which look like snug shorts) to long-sleeved tops and long pants.

Loose-fitting teddies and tap pants were very popular innerwear styles a few years ago, but these days there aren't many on the market. I find them

hard to tuck into pants smoothly, which may be one reason for their decline in popularity. However, they do work better with dresses that don't require a slip. Personally, I prefer a snug-fitting bodysuit or camisole, which can take the place of a bra, instead of these looser styles.

Sleepwear

The large sleepwear category encompasses garments for warm and cool seasons, such as all styles of pajamas, sleepshirts, nightgowns in a wide variety of lengths, and all types of robes, from warm wrapped fleece to light, elegant peignoirs. Teddies reappear in this category as an option for sleepwear. Some women swear by a big, soft T-shirt for sleeping, while others sleep in nothing

at all, but at some point, most women wear sleepwear during the more relaxed, private times of their days.

Loungewear

The last category, loungewear, consists of comfortable garments that you don't actually wear to bed. You change into them when you come home or wear them when you stay at home to announce to yourself and to the world that this is your time. Examples of loungewear include softwear, such as are big, soft tops with matching pull-on pants, and polished pj's with finishing details that enable them to pass for sweats. You're still dressed enough to run out to the mailbox, sign for a package, or say hello to a neighbor, but it's clear you're wearing comfort clothing.

Lingerie Meets Everyday Wear

Several trends have combined to broaden these categories of garments called lingerie. First, clothing designed both for work and for play has become increasingly casual. Originating with corporate "dress-down Fridays," many companies have adopted a less formal style for the rest of the week as well. As workwear goes more casual, loungewear is becoming more polished, so the differences between the two become less and less distinct. I see people dressing more casually both in and out of the office, and the garment categories are meeting somewhere in the middle.

In addition, there's a huge group of workers who rarely dress for the traditional office. For the thousands of people who have home-based businesses or work part time from their homes, the decision whether to dress or not may vary from day to day. If an at-home worker doesn't have an outside appointment, she may wear pj's or a robe in the morning, change into sweats later, or postpone a shower and the responsibility of "dressing" until after she does yoga, bikes, or runs. Sometimes she just never gets around to changing at all.

In recent years, the number of people who work at home has skyrocketed. As a result, loungewear and sleepwear are being worn more than ever, proving to be the garments of choice for many in this group, myself included. For years, I've treasured the freedom to work in goofy pj's. When I was a knitwear designer in Cambridge, Mass., I lived in a large apartment building with my private apartment on the fourth floor and a

This soft, cotton velour polo top makes the perfect stay-at-home loungewear and can just as easily adapt to running to the store for milk.

design studio on the ground floor. I was delighted to discover that late at night, I could skip down the back fire escape from my apartment to work in the studio wearing my big, bright flannel pajamas and no one would see me! (Well, practically no one. After all, there were windows on the back of the building, too.)

There are other ways that the divisions between outerwear and innerwear have become blurred. For example, sports bras are often worn alone as exercisewear for jogging or aerobics.

Make a sturdy, supportive sports bra that's also comfortable by sewing it in two layers of soft cotton/Lycra knit. Worn with matching fitted shorts, the outfit works well for aerobics, jogging, or yoga.

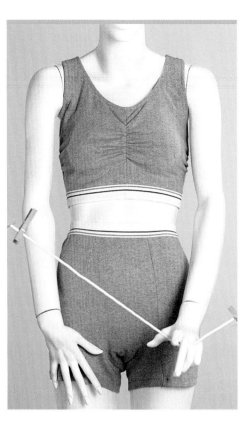

Workout garments can be worn as underwear (I love to wear snug cotton/Lycra workout tops as camisoles and cotton/Lycra dance briefs to hold up my tights), and designers of fine lingerie have long known that many women purchase their elegant nightgowns to be worn as eveningwear.

Lifestyle Loungewear

While many aspects of our lives have grown more frenetic in recent years and stress has become as dangerous a concept as eating eggs once was, we've responded by learning to treasure downtime. We're recognizing that we require rest, that slowing down doesn't equate to laziness, and that there will be plenty of work left to do when we turn our attention back to it. Health has become an individual responsibility.

Try a sports bra, workout top, or fitted camisole with a built-in shelf bra for a versatile garment that can function well under clothing or go it alone during exercise.

Comfort Zone

It's likely that if you had to choose your most comfortable garments, many of them would be lingerie in one form or another. It's not easy to find officewear that's equally comfortable, but recently, several designers have introduced a comfort version of the office skirt—the straight slip-skirt.

Intended to be paired with a jacket or cardigan for work, the skirt is built like a cross between a suit skirt and a half-slip. The waist may include a finished more structured or elastic waistband, while the skirt itself is often made from a brightly printed "daytime" fabric with a lower hem that can include a band of rich, wide lace, like a slip, or a wide border print like the one shown here. This unusual innovation straddles two distinct categories: It feels as if you're wearing a sexy, elegant half-slip, but it is definitely dressed enough to wear out in public, even to the workplace.

And so the category of loungewear has expanded to offer us something to wear during these valued, more private moments. The epitome of "the new loungewear" is a trendy new catalog called Soft Surroundings—Wrap Yourself in Comfort, which is geared to today's stressed-out professional woman. In addition to beautiful, natural-fiber softwear, it sells bed linens, soaps, candles, and home furnishings. What I find most interesting about this catalog is that many of the garment descriptions never say "bed" or "pajama," but instead speak about "linen for lounging," "comfort dressing at its best," and "a soft touch." A softness rating marks each item with one, two, or three clouds. Item descriptions give no clue that we might sleep or rest in these outfits; the only indication is that the woman in the photo is in a relaxed or horizontal position, wearing a soft smile. You can practically smell the flowers and incense. This catalog perfectly represents the meteoric growth of the loungewear category.

Other catalogs feature loungewear paired with other hot trends—healthy living and the environment. The Garnet Hill catalog displays soft, "green" cotton loungewear pieces (called "green" because the fabrics are produced using healthy, environmentally friendly

Since when do pajamas have pockets and a hood? It's not hard to imagine that this cozy, cotton velour pajama set was destined for a life outside the bedroom.

methods). From other companies, I see pages of soft loungewear made from "cotton cashmere," a cotton knit brushed for softness and comfort, and neutrally colored, yoga-style clothing made from natural fibers. These high-quality items are showing up in catalogs because women want and buy them.

Some of the loungewear-style pj's at the top of my list of favorites include soft, baggy, featherweight corduroy pajama pants with an elastic waist and button fly that can easily pass for "real" pants and cotton-knit summer pj's with pull-on shorts and a loosely fitted, button-front top modest enough to answer the door or run out to get the mail. I also like a bright red velour top and pants sold by J. Crew as pj's but built like sweats, including pants pockets and a hood on the boxy, polo-style top (see the photo at left). Frankly, I don't think these pajamas were ever intended for sleeping. Lingerie is finally

The lingerie sections of pattern books hold a wide variety of specialized offerings that can be sewn into beautiful lingerie.

Karen's Closet

In my mind, pajamas have never exclusively meant "bed." Apparently J. Crew had the same idea but took it one step further: Pajamas with style features outside the ordinary, such as pockets, hoods, piping, and topstitching, began showing up in their catalogs. Photos showed soft, brightly colored items worn in unmatched layers with thick socks and unlaced snowboots, and models outdoors amidst piles of snow, carrying firewood. I've never been able to resist comfort, so these pajamas made a big impression on me, influencing my subsequent pj sewing projects.

Outstanding J. Crew examples include orange cotton-flannel pj pants, with the unexpected surprise of pants pockets; I added decorative blue machine embroidery at the hems to coordinate with a favorite shirt. Another favorite is a man's classic navy flannel sleepshirt with white polka dots and red piping.

J. Crew's subsequent offerings became even bolder. A favorite pj set of bright red cotton velour includes pants with pockets and an elastic/drawstring waist, plus a top with a hood (see the top photo on the facing page). Another beloved piece of J. Crew "transition" sleepwear is a pair of featherweight corduroy pants in the most delicious grayed-lavender color with pockets, topstitching, and a button-fly front. These pieces successfully complete the transition from sleepwear to daywear. I've worn both garments boldly out of my house, and no one knows I'm wearing pajamas (although I do look like one of Santa's elves when I wear both of the red pieces together).

seeing daylight, and as a result, there are more choices than ever for us to wear and enjoy the ultimate comfort clothing.

Find Patterns to Please Yourself

Both in the books of the large pattern companies and in small-company brochures and catalogs, you'll find lots of great patterns for lingerie. These garments include everything from gowns and pajamas, traditional shawl-collar and kimono-style robes, and man-style nightshirts and boxers to many choices for bras, camisoles, slips, and a wide variety of panty shapes from thongs to bag-leg pants. Most of these garments have simple shapes and quick, uncomplicated construction. Combined with beautiful fabrics, they make perfect projects for a beginning or intermediate sewer.

Selecting a pattern

When you're ready to choose a pattern, start by browsing through the lingerie sections of the major pattern books. It's also useful to explore smaller, specialty pattern companies, which are often listed in the ad pages of sewing magazines. Some of my favorites are listed in the Resources on p. 135.

Borrow a lingerie pattern from another section of the book. From left: the cap-sleeve tunic makes a cool and comfortable summer pajama top worn with shorts or soft pants; use an oversized shirt pattern for a perfect pajama or loungewear top sewn in cotton, linen, or flannel; a simple, bias-cut blouse makes a stunning nightgown, adapted by drawing the pattern longer and wider to the new hemline, as shown in the illustration at left.

Top-Turned Nightgown

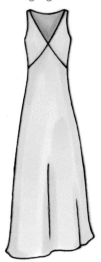

If nothing strikes your fancy in the lingerie section, look through other areas of the catalog, such as Separates, Designer Sportswear, and Dresses. Don't worry that the garment shown isn't exactly what you want; all that matters is the basic shape. If you see a shape that you like, feel free to borrow and adapt it to your use for unique innerwear, sleepwear, or loungewear.

Turning daywear into lingerie

Particularly when choosing a pattern from outside the lingerie section of the catalog, it's likely you'll need to make a few changes to adapt it to your needs. But don't let the idea of changing the pattern scare you. It's usually just a matter of simplifying the style and eliminating details, which can actually make the garment easier and quicker to sew.

Even a pattern for a complicated garment can be simplified by eliminating extra seams, decorative pockets, and

fussy facings. At the neckline, I like to replace the facing with a soft, bias-cut binding or ribbing. If you keep the facings, stitch them to the garment so they stay in place; floppy facings on sleepwear and loungewear can be a bother.

For example, the white linen pajama shirt shown in the photo on the facing page began as a Vogue shirt pattern. I made the style simpler by eliminating the collar and cuffs, making the body a little longer, and adding vents at the sides. The front neck, front edges, and hem are finished with a facing, for

tip. . .

Before sewing, examine your current wardrobe to take stock of which pieces are your favorites and why. Look at the fabric, color, fit, and how well the piece is wearing. Also, figure out why the others don't quite work. These notes will help you decide which features and aspects of a garment you want to include in the lingerie you sew.

which I made a simple pattern by tracing the shirt front onto another sheet of paper and outlining the facing shape and width I wanted for the appliqué effect. I added a narrow strip of bias-cut self-fabric to finish the back neck instead of using a facing there. (You'll find more specifics for this garment on pp. 121–124.)

Other examples are patterns such as Vogue 9772, view A (see the photo and illustration on the facing page). Although it's designed as a sleeveless blouse, it would make a beautiful special-occasion nightgown with its deep V-neckline, graceful diagonal seams, and bias-cut body. For this type of pattern, especially one cut on the bias, make sure you have plenty of ease so the garment will be comfortable and not too clingy.

Vogue pattern 1592 can be made into wonderfully floaty summer pajamas. The tunic's wide neckline and deep front, back, and side slits admit the breeze, and the cap sleeves are cool and comfortable. Because it's described as loose fitting, the tunic probably needs no extra ease and will team up nicely with baggy pj pants or shorts. Cut the pants or shorts in a larger size so they'll be roomy and comfortable.

This white/blue linen pajama shirt started as a blouse pattern but got simpler. After eliminating the collar, cuffs, and back-neck facing and lengthening and widening the body, all that's left is a simple shape that's easy to embellish with appliqué.

Because sleepwear and loungewear need room to be comfortable, always check the amount of ease in a non-lingerie pattern. Plan to add additional ease, especially through the body (bust, waist, and hips), or start with a larger-than-normal size, or both. The easiest way to determine how much ease to add is to compare the pattern measurements with your body and with a similar garment you already enjoy wearing.

By experimenting with styles and patterns from all areas of your closet and all sections of the pattern books, you'll broaden your options for making lingerie that's just what you want. Don't worry about playing by the rules. The more ideas you generate, the more likely you'll be pleased with your results.

Another obvious way to adapt a "daytime" style for sleepwear or loungewear is to choose a softer fabric than the ones suggested on the pattern envelope.

FABRICS AND OTHER THINGS

The materials you select when sewing lingerie make all the difference in the success of your final result—the way the garment looks and feels, how much you enjoy wearing it, how long it lasts, and whether it becomes a treasured favorite. Although the fabric is probably the most important choice you'll make, other decisions such as choosing elastic, lace and other trims, needles, and thread will also have an impact on the success of the finished garment.

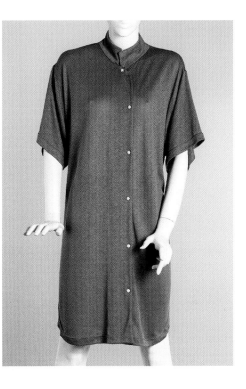

Choosing a Great Fabric

Naturally, choosing which fabrics to use for a given garment is a matter of personal preference. As sewers, what we really want is the right to choose! The greatest advantage of sewing your own lingerie is that you can have exactly what you want. Knits and other fabrics that stretch make a lot of sense, especially for smoothly fitted lingerie. But the decision is up to you: If you prefer to wear nothing but silk against your skin, you can do just that.

When selecting fabric for a lingerie project, think of how you want to feel when you wear it. Should the garment be huge, warm, and cozy? Thin and sleek to fit invisibly under fluid garments? Or supple and elegant for those special occasions when you want to feel gorgeous? The right fabric will help create the feel and function you want. Think about another similar garment you've loved and what kind of fabric made it such a pleasure, then let your imagination take over. If you see an unusual fabric and wonder if it'd be great for lingerie, the answer is yes—if you like the feel of it, chances are it'll be wonderful. Sewing your own lingerie is all about comfort, pleasure, and choice, so it's all up to you.

Beyond the traditional

Just a few years ago, a discussion of fabrics for sewing lingerie would have included the usual nylon tricots and sheers, brushed nylon for winter gowns, and perhaps a few cotton knits. I have a Vogue/Butterick sewing booklet from the early '70s called "Sewing with Special Fabrics—Lingerie." Believe it or not, the only fabrics it mentions are eight different weights and types of nylon tricot plus stretch lace.

These days, taking a cue from ready-to-wear, the range of fabrics suitable for lingerie has expanded to include practically every type of fabric. Tricot still serves as a mainstay of inexpensive ready-to-wear lingerie, but I find that natural fibers like cotton and silk offer greater comfort and breathability, and Lycra blends give a smoother fit. Beyond these fabrics, a vast array of other options exists, from linen to velour and silk chiffon to synthetic fleece.

You'll find that the wide variety of fabrics used in ready-to-wear lingerie is also accessible to those of us who want to sew it ourselves. So when browsing in fabric stores, remember that any fabric that serves the purpose can and should be pressed into service for innerwear, sleepwear, and loungewear.

Open your mind when you think of fabrics for lingerie. Just about any fabric that feels good against your skin can be used successfully for lingerie. In this chapter, I'll take a look at some of the numerous fabric possibilities. Also, refer to pp. 94–95 for a discussion of additional fabrics that work well for bras.

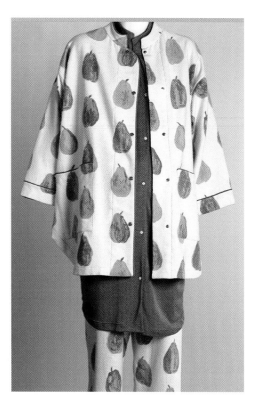

In chilly weather, layer several cozy pajama/loungewear pieces for relaxed comfort. The soft kiwi knit first layer (shown underneath) is intended for sleeping; add the warm flannel "jacket" and pants to make a perfect at-home work ensemble.

Where to look

Finding beautiful and interesting fabrics has become one of the most challenging aspects of sewing today. Quite a few of the independent fabric stores that specialized in better-quality fabrics are no longer in business, so you have to learn to dig for the fabrics you want. And be willing to pay more for fabrics of the highest quality—they're worth it! Just because a fabric like silk seersucker isn't sold in your local fabric store doesn't mean it's not available. Local stores generally focus on selling fabrics that a large number of sewers in their areas want to buy.

So don't limit yourself just to the local fabric stores. Shop there first, of course, but if you don't see what you want, try accessing some of the outstanding fabric stores that sell by mail order and on the Internet. Some stores stock nearly every fabric under the sun, while others specialize in obscure and hard-to-find fabrics.

Selling by mail allows stores to reach a larger audience, so they can build and maintain the volume they need to stay in business without having to rely on walk-in traffic only. If you're willing to put up with time delays and making decisions from samples instead of fondling yardage (which we all love to do), buying by mail can open up a whole world of fabrics. Your search may not yield many bolts of silk seersucker, but you'll feel as if you're uncovering buried treasure when you find just one that's gorgeous.

Before shopping for fabrics, always check the directions on the envelope of the pattern you're considering. There you'll find suggested fabrics appropriate

Stores that sell designer offcuts tend to have high-quality fabrics at great prices. However, their stock changes rapidly and often cannot be reordered, so be specific about what you want when requesting samples, and act quickly after receiving them. Compile your own list of favorite fabric stores and other resources. Meanwhile, check out my list of suppliers in the Resources on p. 135.

Wearing Your Sheets to Bed

If you're searching for silky, high-quality cotton fabric or thick, soft flannel and can't find a color or print you like, consider cutting your garment from an unorthodox source—bed sheets. Beautiful sheets are available in many stores and catalogs, and frequent sales make the prices affordable. One king-size sheet is the equivalent of 6 yd. of 50-in.-wide fabric, providing more than enough fabric for the pear-print flannel pajama shirt and pants shown in the top photo on the facing page (sheet purchased from the Garnet Hill catalog).

A word of caution about printed sheets: When choosing, consider the scale of the print on your body. Prints designed for bed sheets may differ in scale from those designed for garments; after all, a bed is a larger "canvas" than a body. So what looks like a manageable print in a photo may, in fact, overwhelm your frame. The pear print is a bold size for a garment, but the soft watercolors of the print make it work. If possible, hold the sheet up to your body in front of a mirror to evaluate the effect before cutting into your sheet.

When adapting a purchased bed sheet as fabric for sleepwear, beware of prints that are too large or bold. At right, the softly colored cloud print would be perfect for pajamas, while the contrasting cow print at left might overwhelm.

for that particular style, and if it says "knits only" or "unsuitable for obvious diagonals," pay attention to the designer's comments—they're there for a reason. Patterns created especially for knits and stretch fabrics generally include less ease than those for straight-grain woven fabrics and may have fewer darts and less shaping.

Whenever you decide to substitute another type of fabric, be aware that you may need to make adjustments in order for that fabric to work. And if you're a new or less-than-confident sewer, it's a good idea to stick with the fabric recommendations on the envelope, at least at first.

Traditional Fabric Options

I'm sure that a century ago most lingerie was sewn from fine cotton, linen, and silk. But when I say traditional, I'm referring to the lingerie fabrics that most American women have worn since the 1950s, fabrics that came into popu-

larity during and after World War II. This category includes tricot and other nylons, Lycra, some cotton knits for innerwear, and cotton wovens such as batiste, chenille, and flannelette for sleepwear, with woven silks reserved for special-occasion lingerie. Most are easy-to-sew, wash-and-wear fabrics, although the more delicate silks respond better to handwashing.

Knits

Soft, fluid knits are perfect for lingerie, especially innerwear that will be worn under other garments. But for some reason, many perfectly capable sewers still shy away from sewing knits. The truth is that stable knits can be some of the easiest fabrics to sew. Most have edges that don't ravel, so they don't even require extra finishing.

The main requirement for sewing knits is that the seams need to stretch with the fabric. As long as you sew with a zigzag, serger, or other stretch stitch,

Natural-fiber knits are versatile staples for all types of lingerie. Shown here from left are a fun, all-cotton insect print; a luxuriously fluid kiwi knit of rayon and linen; a lustrous, high-quality cotton knit from Europe; a comfortable violet cotton/Lycra; and another European cotton knit.

Comfort Zone

I'm sure that when nylon was developed in 1938 as the first completely synthetic fiber, it was revolutionary. Welcomed as a substitute for the silk that was in short supply during the war, nylon tricot quickly became a staple in women's lingerie. Yet despite its continued popularity, many women today find that tricot feels clammy against the skin, especially in warm weather, because it doesn't breathe well or absorb moisture.

Now that we have such a wide choice of fabrics available, there's no reason to limit our lingerie sewing to tricot. The ideal lingerie fabrics are soft, stretchy, and comfortable, as well as absorbent and breathable. In fact, if you're going to invest your time in sewing, I suggest that you make something of high quality, like the better lingerie found in department stores. Luckily, we have plenty of alternatives—we can sew just what we want.

or if you stretch the fabric slightly as you sew with a straight stitch, you can get beautiful results. If you'd like to learn more about sewing with knits, I recommend the book *Sewing with Knits* by Connie Long (The Taunton Press, 2000).

Nylon tricot Probably the best-known and most commonly used lingerie fabric, nylon tricot is suitable for many everyday innerwear garments. It's thin and smooth under clothing, relatively low cost, and virtually indestructible. Tricot is so tough, in fact, that it's hard on scissors, pins, and machine needles (you'll notice that needles will dull quickly, so replace your needle after every few tricot garments). Tricot yardage is available in a variety of styles, from sheer to satin tricot, and many home-sewing instructions for lingerie have focused on this traditional fabric.

Spandex For decades, spandex has been a staple in bra and girdle construction. But the heavy, rubbery spandex of yesteryear is quite different from the thin, lightweight knit and woven Lycra (DuPont's brand name for spandex) fabrics we have available today. The key to spandex's appeal, both then and now, is not only comfortable stretch but also recovery. The fabric regains its original shape after being stretched over and over again. The amount of stretch in a Lycra-blend fabric varies widely, from 25 percent or less to 100 percent or more. Patterns designed for Lycra-blend fabrics specify how much stretch is needed for the correct fit.

Cotton knits Cotton knits have long been a popular option for panties. I fondly remember Carter's "spanky pants" with wide, comfortable leg bands that we all wore as kids. But looking

tip. . .

Cut edges on nylon tricot and other single knits tend to curl, which can make them tricky to handle. Laceland (www.laceland.com) offers this tip: Fold the fabric yardage in four layers over a hanger, and spray the surface with liquid starch. After it's dry, lay out and cut the fabric as usual. The starch adds body and stabilizes the edges, then easily washes out before wearing.

Woven fabrics can make outstanding lingerie. From left: two examples of a new breed of fabric, wovens with Lycra stretch, in a cream silk ottoman and a white cotton piqué; yellow pure-silk seersucker; a cool cotton mesh with eyelet embroidery; and a cotton jacquard with a woven sailboat design that would make a perfect summer pajama.

back, these knits often felt thick and bagged out of shape quickly, and clothes tended to cling to them. The emergence of thinner, more fluid cotton knits and cotton/Lycra blends has made it possible to sew cotton lingerie that's sleekly fitted yet still extremely comfortable. A small percentage of Lycra is all it takes—many of the current knit fabrics contain 92 percent cotton with 8 percent or less of Lycra. These fabrics often have a smooth, fine finish that reduces clinging. And you'll also find some beautiful, silky, all-cotton rib knits that stretch and contour to the body luxuriously.

Cotton knits are also perfect for sleeping. The day-to-day sleepwear of choice for many women is a soft, oversized (and well-worn!) T-shirt. In sweltering weather, try a short, loose-fitting cotton knit summer gown with narrow straps; it's the coolest garment you can find, if you have to wear something.

Of course, the ultimate cotton knits are the luxurious ones imported from Europe, often Austria or Switzerland. They're silky, tightly knitted interlock fabrics with an elegant sheen and stable cut edges. If you haven't yet sewn with

this superior type of fabric, give it a try. The price is higher but definitely worth it, especially since a yard of fabric can make several pairs of panties (depending on size and style), and each piece would sell for $16 to $28 in better stores and catalogs such as Garnet Hill.

Wovens

Woven fabrics also play an essential role in lingerie. What can be more comfortable than thick, cotton flannel pajamas in the winter and fine, cotton batiste or seersucker ones in the summer? Wovens tend to be easy to sew, although they generally require more seam finishing than knits, especially for fabrics that ravel, such as linen, rayon, and many silks. Even though most wovens don't stretch, you can cut them on the bias if you'd like a close fit that's still stretchy and comfortable. And you'll find a growing group of wovens available with Lycra blended in, so that you get comfy stretch and shape retention without using a bias cut.

Flannel and flannelette Traditional favorites for warm pajamas and robes, cotton flannel and flannelette are comfy

and affordable. Flannelette is a lighter-weight fabric that's often sold in pastel solids, small florals, and playful prints for children's clothing and sleepwear. The alternative is beefier cotton flannel, often available in rich solids and in yarn-dyed plaids and checks (yarn-dyeing indicates a superior fabric, since the color is woven into the fabric instead of just printed on). Another variety of cotton flannel, called chamois cloth, is a thick, densely napped fabric intended for men's casual winter shirts, but it also works well for toasty sleepwear and loungewear.

Cotton chenille Cotton chenille is a classic for comfortable, absorbent, everyday bathrobes and also works well for soft pajama shirts, although it can be difficult to find as yardage these days. Cotton chenille has a long, furry

The perfect robe for a hot summer day: The furry pile on soft cotton chenille cushions and absorbs moisture to keep you cool.

Wrap yourself in thick, deeply napped cotton flannel for a snug cold-weather pajama or robe. The gray check is a yarn-dyed woven, while the watercolor pear is a print.

pile that's woven in patterns like stripes and florals, typically in the same color as the background fabric. Because it's so absorbent, chenille is the perfect fabric to wear after a shower. Some of the best ready-to-wear cotton chenille robes in stores are made in Australia, so let's hope that country will export some of its fabrics to us as well.

Less Predictable Fabric Choices

If sewers are taking their cue from ready-to-wear, it makes sense to broaden the list of fabrics that are appropriate for lingerie. The traditional fabrics are all wonderful choices, but if you're looking for something a little different, consider one of the fabrics discussed here. From unexpected natural fibers to the latest high-tech synthetics, the requirements remain the same—the fabric has to be comfortable. When you start to work with these newer fabrics for lingerie, you'll find most of them just as easy to sew as traditional lingerie fabrics, if not easier.

Natural fibers

Natural fibers, so called because they're derived from natural plant and animal

High-tech fabrics designed for performance outerwear easily adapt for making beautiful lingerie. From top: cantaloupe and periwinkle Bipolar Mesh, lime Polartec 100 thermal piqué, and teal Supplex nylon/Lycra knit.

sources, are great for lingerie. They breathe, are absorbent, and tend to feel comfortable on the skin. Some good natural-fiber alternatives include:

Corduroy. All-cotton, featherweight corduroy is soft and wonderful for cozy pajamas that can double as at-home loungewear.

Cotton velour. Often blended with 20 percent polyester, soft cotton velour makes wonderful robes and warm, versatile pj's that can look and function like sweats.

Linen. A century ago, linen was the standard for fine bedding and sleepwear. For summer, fine handkerchief linen still makes beautifully cool and comfortable pajamas, if you don't mind a few wrinkles and rumples. Wash and dry the fabric several times before sewing for a softer, more natural finish.

Luxury silk fabrics

For special lingerie, there are relatively expensive and delicate luxury woven fabrics, such as silk chiffon, satin, silk crepe in various weights, and beautiful woven silk jacquards, that tend to be overlooked. These fabrics may or may not play a large role in your everyday lingerie, but it's fun to have a couple of gorgeous pieces in your wardrobe. So don't limit your choices—scan all the fabrics in a store for the most beautiful options. Plan to spend time on a few exquisite finishing details (see chapter 6) for the ultimate garment that's a pleasure to wear.

You can also use silk for everyday garments if you like. In the past, silk fabrics were popular only for the wealthy minority who could afford very expensive garments. But these days, with the many affordable silks available and the option of prewashing silk for a softly rumpled look, sewing a wardrobe of silk lingerie doesn't have to be either expensive or high maintenance. Soft, washed silk breathes and feels wonderful against the skin.

If you'd like to use a woven silk for a close-fitting undergarment like a camisole, panty, or slip, choose a thin, fluid fabric such as crepe or georgette or one with a little more body such as silk broadcloth, jacquard, or seersucker. Consider cutting the fabric on the bias for comfort. A bias-cut undergarment requires a little more fabric and some special handling during construction, but it feels great and flexes as your body moves for a better fit without sacrificing comfort.

High-tech fabrics

The term "high-tech" refers to fabrics developed and refined using complex human-made fibers and processes. Many high-tech garment fabrics are comfortable to wear, easy to sew, durable, and reasonably priced. New fabrics are being developed and perfected every year, emerging first in ready-to-wear and then trickling down into fabric stores, so be on the lookout for new and improved fabric forms.

Some of the best high-tech fabrics I've found include:

Polarfleece. For many fussy natural-fiber purists like me, high-quality polyester fleece has revolutionized our thinking on synthetics. This is the first all-polyester fabric I've ever loved without reservation. There's nothing so cozy on a damp, chilly day as a layer of soft, warmth-absorbing Polarfleece. You've probably seen it used for warm winter robes, but would you consider it for a bra? Recently, I came across a beautifully fluid, soft, and cozy bra made from Polartec 100. This thin fabric is the lightweight "little sister" of the Polartec 200 we love for sweaters and lightweight jackets and the heavier Polartec 300 used for outerwear. It's a comfortable, indoor-weight fleece that is also great made up as a blouse or turtleneck.

Crushed polyester/Lycra velour. I've seen some comfy-looking bras and camisoles made from lustrous, crushed polyester/Lycra velour. Synthetic velours tend to have a soft, rich texture and lots of stretch, up to 100 percent. The category of knitted, synthetic velours is one that will continue to grow and expand, and these fabrics work quite well for many lingerie styles.

Nylon/Lycra and microfiber knits. Some of the new, thin nylon/Lycra and microfiber knits are ideal fabrics for lingerie. In ready-to-wear, you'll see these fabrics in lingerie at J. Crew and Banana Republic, and they're also available as yardage for the home sewer. Keep your eyes open for new versions, especially in stores that sell designer offcuts.

At Banksville Fabrics in Norwalk, Conn., I found a great fabric called elastine that's fluid and has a matte finish with lots of stretch. It's shown in the photo on p. 24 layered with stretch lace for a camisole and panty. Sheer nylon/Lycra and nylon/Lycra satin are

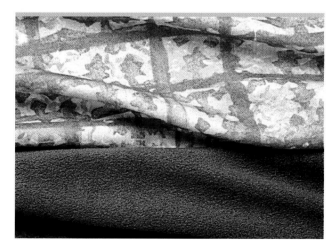

Wearing Polartec is like enjoying a hot cup of tea on a cold day: It provides cozy warmth that's just right. Shown here are a Polartec 100 microfleece one-sided print and a Polartec 100 fleece solid.

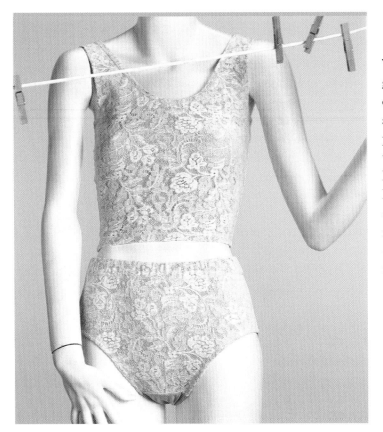

One woman's ideal everyday lingerie. Although each person has her own ideas of perfection, for the author this smooth, simple Lycra-blend knit set is made to order.

Woven fabrics with Lycra. The emergence of high-tech woven fabrics blended with Lycra results in wovens that stretch, making them comfortable and practical for lingerie, even when cut on the straight grain. These fabrics typically have crosswise stretch but none lengthwise, so be sure to place the stretch going around the body for comfort. Look for both silk/Lycra and cotton/Lycra blends as well as synthetics. I've used a silk/Lycra ottoman for an elegant, special-occasion beaded and embroidered bra (shown at the left in the photo on p. 86), and I've also found a white cotton/Lycra piqué that will make a great bra or camisole.

Selecting the Right Trims and Notions

At the same time that you're searching for wonderful fabrics, it's a good idea to consider the other materials you'll need for a project. Before you begin sewing, check that you have essential notions, such as elastic and thread, and the right needles. Also, you may want to add lace, ribbon, or beads as trim or decorative elements.

The more you know about the various types of elastic, stretch and stable laces, and decorative elements such as ribbon and beads, the better the choices you'll be able to make for each specific garment you plan. I suggest that you buy some of each type that interests you and make samples with each one, following the instructions in chapter 3. Then, when planning a new garment, you can browse through your samples to find the choices that will work best.

both perfect for bras. You'll also find new fabrics with brand names such as Coolmax, Bi Polar, and Supplex/Lycra in stores that specialize in outerwear fabrics, such as The Rain Shed (see Resources on p. 135), where some styles are sold as a wicking or moisture-absorbing liner for outerwear or for long underwear. Describe what you want and how you plan to use it, so stores will send you the correct samples.

Stretch lace. Lace yardage that contains Lycra works well for soft, comfortable lingerie. Most are nylon/Lycra blends, although I found an especially beautiful piece that has a cottony feel (see the photo above). Although its fiber content wasn't noted on the bolt, I believe it's either acetate or acrylic blended with Lycra.

Elastics

Sewers tend to view elastic in a critical light, since it's often the first area to wear out on a garment. But when you think of how hard elastic works, how often it's required to stretch out for hours and then bounce back to shape, you realize how amazingly durable this stuff is. It's truly the functional "backbone" of many lingerie garments.

The wide variety of elastics available works well for all kinds of lingerie. Which elastic you choose is largely a matter of personal preference. Some are strong and easy to handle but thicker, while others are very stretchy, thinner, and sleeker. Test each one so you know what you like and can make the best choice for each new garment.

Most sewers are familiar with general types of elastic such as polyester woven and braided elastics, nonroll elastic, natural cotton/rubber swimwear elastic (which tends to be a bit thick but is long lasting), and thin, clear polyurethane-tape elastic (which is slippery to sew but gives a nice, flat finish on panty legs). For lingerie, these types of regular garment elastic work very well in my favorite covered applications where the elastic doesn't touch the skin.

Flat elastics range in width from ¼ in. to 2 in. You can also buy round and cord elastics and elastic thread, which don't have as many applications for lingerie. Most of these elastics are available in limited colors, typically black and white and sometimes natural.

Karen's Closet

One of my favorite camisoles, which I made from high-tech nylon/Lycra velour, was modeled after a ready-to-wear camisole I bought at J. Crew. Made from a smooth, nylon/Lycra knit, the J. Crew camisole was perfect in every way—it had a snug, supportive fit, was the perfect length for me (ending just at the waist), and had skinny straps of bra-strap elastic with rings and adjusters to give it that authentic lingerie feeling.

Once at home, I examined my purchase more closely and realized how easy it would be to sew a similar one. The camisole is basically a simple tube shape, scooped a bit lower in back, and finished at the top with a band of stretch lace and twin-needle hemmed at the bottom. Easy straps of narrow strap elastic with adjusters complete the camisole. I made mine from brown floral-print nylon/Lycra velour that's a little more interesting than the original solid black. It's not only beautiful and simple to make but also very soft and comfortable to wear.

LAUNDRY DAY

A trip through the washer and quick line-drying is the best care method for lingerie, since the dryer spells trouble for fabrics, especially elastics and blends containing Lycra.

Since lingerie is washed and worn more than any other type of clothing, you want to make sure your sewing efforts will stand up to the laundry methods you use. Let's face it, once you create a garment you love, you want it to last as long as possible. For best results, I suggest a combination of careful prewashing and gentle care methods that are kind to your garment and help to prolong its useful life.

My less-than-mainstream position on gentle laundering practically eliminates one of the major pieces of laundry equipment: the dryer. I've found that very few fabrics improve with machine drying. The continuous friction combined with the dryer's heat breaks down fibers, causing them to wear out more quickly. So if you love a garment and want it to last, avoid the dryer. And for many garments, you really don't have a choice: Silks easily get fried in the dryer, and heat shortens the life of elastics and any fabric containing Lycra.

For most garments that you've spent the time and trouble to make, a trip through the washing machine on a normal or delicate cycle followed by quick line-drying is the best plan. If you live in a cold climate, try placing a wooden drying rack in the room with your furnace. It takes only a few extra minutes to shake out and smooth wet garments and lay them on the rack, and most

clothing will dry overnight in these conditions. For fabrics like corduroy and cotton flannel that become stiff when line-dried, a 10-minute tumble in the dryer removes wrinkles before folding.

Prewashing

Before starting a sewing project, prewash the yardage by laundering it as you plan to care for the finished garment so any shrinkage will happen before you cut out the garment. An exception to my dryer rule: I do use the dryer when prewashing many fabrics before sewing. I find that this single trip through the dryer often helps to thicken, soften, and stabilize many fabrics. This also allows me the freedom to use the dryer later in a pinch, if I'm leaving town or just need a garment in a hurry.

Some cotton knits, like sweatshirt fleece and cotton/Lycra blends, may continue to shrink for the first two or three washings, so you may want to treat them several times before cutting out. Also, washed linen used for lingerie benefits from several washer/dryer trips for a softly rumpled effect.

If you're making an elegant robe from silk jacquard or cotton velvet, you may want to dry-clean it. But personally, I prefer to hand-wash most silks and luxury fabrics if doing so doesn't alter the fabric too much. Before you decide whether to wash a special piece of fabric, test the results on a ⅛-yd. strip or 6-in. by 6-in. swatch of the fabric. Write down the measurements of the swatch, then wash, dry, and press it; measure again. If the color bleeds unacceptably, if the fabric shrinks too much, or if you don't like the washed effect, plan to dry-clean the finished garment.

How to handwash

It may seem silly to offer instructions on how to handwash a garment, but I find that many people rely so thoroughly on their multiple-cycle heavy-duty-to-delicate machines that they rarely handwash a piece anymore.

Handwashing may seem like a hassle, but it actually takes just a few minutes, and it's the gentlest way to clean a delicate garment without filling it with dry-cleaning fumes. It's also an easy way to make sure any soiled spots are removed so you don't have to wash the piece all over again. Personally, I find a row of carefully handwashed sweaters, hanging to dry on my wooden rack, to be oddly satisfying.

When handwashing, use a mild soap or detergent. Some swear by Orvus or Z'Out, but I prefer a squirt of mild liquid dishwashing detergent like Palmolive or Ivory. If you're washing silk, the best choice is shampoo, since silk and hair are both protein fibers. Prespot or work on any soiled areas before immersing the garment, since spots will be harder to locate once it's wet.

Half-fill a sink or plastic tub with warm water, adding a small amount of soap while it's filling (remember, the more you use, the longer you'll have to rinse). Slosh the soap around to dissolve it, then add the garment, wetting the fabric thoroughly, and let it soak for 5 to 10 minutes. Check any prespotted areas to make sure they've come clean, then empty the soapy water from the tub and refill it with clean, tepid water. Gently swish the fabric around, and repeat the rinse step until no soap residue is left.

Pour out the final rinse water, then press the fabric on the side of the tub to remove the excess. For a delicate garment, carefully lift and lay it on a towel, fold the towel over the garment, and press out the water to prevent the weight of the water from distorting the fabric when you hang it. Smooth out the wrinkles and reshape the piece. You can dry pieces flat on a towel, but I find that this setup takes longer to dry. Most pieces can hang on a hanger or over a wooden bar, which offers more support, and will dry quickly. For sturdier pieces, my favorite way to banish excess water is to spin them briefly in the washing machine's spin cycle, then smooth and hang them over a bar.

For making lingerie, you can use many types of everyday elastics in covered applications. Clockwise from top: natural cotton/rubber swimwear elastic; polyester braid elastic in two widths and two colors; and clear polyurethane tape elastic.

In addition, there are elastics designed specifically for lingerie that tend to be softer and work well in applications where the elastic is exposed. They include:

Lingerie elastic. This elastic is soft and less irritating to the skin, allowing it to be applied with the elastic exposed. Lingerie elastic is available in a variety of widths and typically has one picot or scalloped edge, which can create a delicate edge on the finished garment.

Latex-free lingerie elastic. This soft elastic is available for those whose skin is sensitive to latex.

Plush elastic. Plush elastic is used to finish the edges of a bra, but it can also work well in other areas where the elastic will be exposed to the skin. Its brushed or felted inner surface makes it comfortable to wear, and it often has one picot edge.

Strap elastic. Having minimal stretch and typically plush or felted on one or both sides, strap elastic allows a strap to give but offers more support than other elastics.

Fold-over elastic. Fold-over elastic often appears in ready-to-wear lingerie, where it may finish the upper edges of a snug-fitting camisole and also form the straps. Designed to fold over and finish a raw edge, it has a satiny surface and a crease line at the center.

You'll find lingerie elastics in black, white, and ecru, plus a limited range of fashion colors. Elastics can also be dyed with the finished garment, as described on pp. 112–115.

Special soft lingerie elastics can be sewn so that they're exposed to the skin. Clockwise from top: striped men's underwear elastic; fold-over elastic; lingerie elastics with a picot edge; plush strap elastic; and elastic with one eyelet edge.

For a variety of elastic application methods, see the instructions on pp. 46–54. If you plan to sew lingerie frequently, order catalogs from several of the lingerie suppliers listed in Resources on p. 135; request samples from each company because the stock at each one varies. Purchase several types of elastic that interest you so you can make a set of reference samples. In addition to fabrics, these invaluable suppliers also sell bra underwires and channeling, closures, slides and rings for straps, and garters for sewing bras and other lingerie.

An elegant lace can beautifully trim a simple piece of lingerie. From top: four examples of narrow cotton lace, some with a touch of nylon, followed by three nylon or polyester laces.

Lace

Some people love lingerie lavished with lace. I prefer the simpler, classic style of cotton laces over the more "lacey" synthetic ones. Either way, lace can be used to neatly finish an edge or as an embellishment. Make whatever style pleases you. If you enjoy wearing lace, there are many elegant lace trims available, and they can add a beautiful touch to your lingerie without much extra effort.

Lace is available in several fibers and blends including nylon, cotton/nylon, and Lycra blends, as well as in a variety of widths and in many designs, mostly florals. There are some that stretch and some that don't; use whatever is appropriate for the garment you're working on. For example, if your garment is fitted and the fabric stretchy, you'll probably want to use stretch lace so it will flex with the garment. Stretch lace trim is the perfect finish at the top edge of a stretch-velour camisole. To trim a

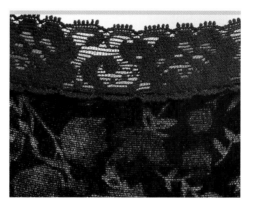

Stretch lace creates a very easy finished edge on a stretchy garment like this polyester/Lycra velour camisole. Attach the lace with a zigzag stitch so the seam will stretch, too.

woven camisole, the hem of a slip, or another garment area that isn't required to stretch, you can use a nonstretch lace, like the narrow cotton lace that finishes the hem of the silk seersucker camisole and slip shown in the photo on p. 14. Either way, lace can be used to create a flexible, finished look with very little effort. In chapter 3, I'll describe a few methods for applying lace trims.

When I was searching for stretch lace to finish the edges of a cream cotton lace camisole, I found a lace I loved, but it was only available in white. Since I needed it in cream, the easy solution was to brew a cup of strong black tea, allow it to cool slightly, then immerse the lace in the teacup. After an hour or less, I removed and rinsed the lace. The color, which turned out lighter when dry, was permanent.

Ribbon and beads

Although it may look complex, it's not difficult to create incredibly delicate trims using ribbon and beads. I generally reserve this type of embellishment for very special garments, but you could also use these details on a more playful, casual piece if it suits you.

Silk ribbon is available in a variety of widths (2mm, 4mm, 7mm, and 13mm) and in more than 200 solid, variegated, and hand-dyed colors. You can also dye your own shades. You'll find beautiful seed beads in various sizes from 10 to 15 (beads become smaller as the number grows larger) in just about every color imaginable. To give you an idea of bead size, about 18 size 11 beads, placed end to end, measure 1 in.

I suggest that you handwash any garments with either silk ribbon or seed beads, so match your choice of trims to the way you plan to care for the finished garment. For a more durable, everyday garment, polyester satin or other synthetic ribbon would be a better choice. See pp. 126–134 for instructions on several ways to apply silk ribbon and beads.

Needles and thread

Because lingerie fabrics tend to be tightly knitted or woven, I suggest sewing lingerie with a relatively small needle and fine thread, which helps to avoid distorting the fabric. Beyond that, the needle and thread you choose depend on the type of fabric you're sewing. Try a size 80/12 needle for velour, chenille, and French terry, and a finer size 70/10 or 60/8 needle for silks and fine fabrics. Use a ballpoint, universal, or stretch needle for knits. As always, use the smallest, sharpest sewing-machine needle that works with your fabric and thread.

For constructing most lingerie garments, my choice is a high-quality filament-polyester thread that's smooth, strong, and resilient, such as Gütermann or Mettler Metrosene. If you're sewing with lightweight tricot and sheers, you may want to try an extra-fine polyester/cotton thread, such as Coats & Clark Dual Duty Plus machine-embroidery thread. And for

Used sparingly, silk or synthetic ribbon and a sprinkling of beads can delicately embellish a special lingerie garment.

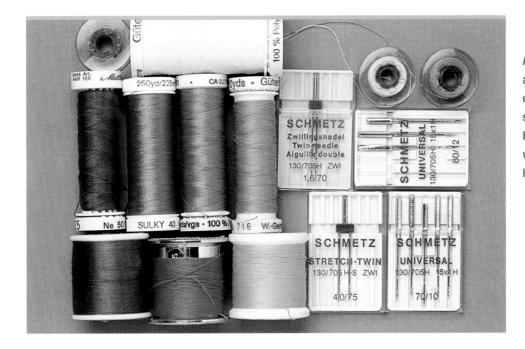

Assorted threads such as long-staple polyester filament and small-size needles, both single and twin, work well for sewing lingerie.

delicate natural fiber fabrics such as silk chiffon, I suggest a cotton machine-embroidery thread like Mettler silk-finish mercerized cotton thread. If your thread is too heavy, it will add too much thickness to the seams; if the thread is too light, it can break when the seam flexes.

For decorative stitching, you can choose from an enormous variety of threads available for machine embroidery. A fine cotton machine-embroidery thread like the Mettler silk-finish makes it easier to sew smooth, even satin-stitching. For the lustrous embroidery on the charcoal silk bra shown in the photo on p. 86, I used Sulky 40 rayon thread, which comes in many colors and has a beautiful sheen.

Don't we all love to sew because we're crazy about fabric? With so many incredible fabrics and embellishments to choose from, even the planning becomes fun. Once you've selected a fabric, trims, and thread for your garment, you're ready to fit the pattern to your body.

Before you begin to sew, always test the needle, thread, stitch length, and tension on samples of your fabric, and make adjustments until you're happy with the seam. Change to a new needle every few garments or whenever your stitches start to skip or your needle strikes a pin.

THE BEST SEWING TECHNIQUES

When sewing lingerie, as with most other types of sewing, having a wide variety of options and techniques at your disposal will help you to sew better, more beautiful garments. In my opinion, there's no right or wrong way to accomplish a specific task; many suitable options exist. Which one to choose depends on the fabric, the look you want, and maybe even on your mood that day. By becoming familiar with the many options for sewing lingerie seams and edges, for applying elastics, and for closures, you'll have a range of techniques at hand when you're ready to make these decisions.

The quickest and easiest way to become familiar with these options is to make a series of samples before you even begin to sew a garment. Sampling is an easy way to save yourself a lot of time and trouble. It's a no-risk way to investigate how your seams, edge finishes, and elastic applications will look and feel before you attempt them on your final product. Especially when you are venturing into a new type of sewing or learning a new technique, a set of basic samples can serve as a reference library to draw on whenever you need to make decisions about a new project.

Making and labeling samples of stitches and sewing techniques will give you the specific information you need, allow you a chance to work out any details, and leave you with the confidence to choose the technique for the next garment you sew.

Good samples can banish nearly all the worries you have about starting a new piece, as well as eliminate many of those well-intentioned garments that turn out to be disappointments. So don't be limited by the suggestions in your pattern guide sheet. These instructions are often just a bare-bones approach to constructing the garment. By studying ready-to-wear and making samples, you'll see that there are a variety of suitable ways to accomplish the same task, some of which enhance the garment and are more pleasing than others.

Good Sewing Starts with the Right Equipment

You don't need special equipment to sew great lingerie. But in general, the better your machine works, the more fun you'll have sewing. If your equipment has useful features, makes perfect stitches, and is tuned and adjusted properly, sewing will be less frustrating and the job will be completed quickly and with less swearing.

If you haven't already done so, make it a goal to educate yourself about sewing machines, sergers, irons and boards, and other options by reading, talking with friends (the Internet is a good place to read and ask questions of other sewers), and testing machines at dealers' shops. Buy the best equipment you can afford, and keep it in excellent condition, tuned and ready to roll. An expensive sewing machine won't make you a sewing expert, but a poorly cared for clunker will definitely hold you back.

A serger offers a quick way to sew lingerie at home. Its clean-finished, stretchy seams are ideal for lingerie garments. Ready-to-wear lingerie is typically constructed with serged seams, so a serger can give your garments a professional look. It also comes in handy for straight-grain garments cut from ravely fabrics, since it quickly joins and finishes the cut edges in one pass.

But you don't have to own a serger to sew beautiful lingerie. Most of the garments shown in this book were constructed without a serger. For sewing on knits, a simple, narrow zigzag stitch gives you soft, stretchy seams; having a few overlock stitches on your sewing machine is useful, too. You can get great results with a sewing machine alone.

Whichever equipment you use, test your machine on scraps of the fabric before you begin sewing the garment, and make adjustments until you're happy with the stitch and the seam.

Use this chapter to create your own lingerie sample set. To get started, dig out your fabric remnants or purchase small amounts of the fabrics you plan to work with and buy the findings and elastics you'll need. Make samples of the seam finishes that interest you, the elastic applications that sound appealing, and hems and edges you like. Be sure to label them, so you'll remember exactly what you did. On a hang tag or slip of paper pinned to the sample, label each with the pertinent data about how you made it (including stitch choice, length, width, tension, needle, thread, elastic, process), and then stash them for easy reference.

When you're ready to sew a new piece, take out the samples, feel your new fabric, and use your observations to make the best choices about how to proceed with your project. You'll save time, avoid mistakes, and increase your confidence, all at the same time.

Seam and Edge Finishes

There are a number of options for sewing strong, flexible lingerie seams and smoothly finished edges, many of which you will have used before on other garments. Your best choice for each task depends on the type of garment you're making, the fabric, and the look you want, so make samples of each one. Following are some options for seams and edges that will enhance the quality of your sewn lingerie.

Choices for everyday seams

Your lingerie is only as strong as its seams, and for stretchy fabrics, seams

A three-thread serger stitch creates a strong, stretchy seam or edge that's quick to sew and works well on both knits and wovens. Use the right needle position, as shown for the stitch at top, for narrow seams on delicate fabrics. *(Photo by Scott Phillips, © The Taunton Press, Inc.)*

need to be especially strong. Which seam you choose depends on your fabric, the garment's function, and the equipment you have available. If time is of the essence, note that some seams take less time to sew than others, requiring only one row of stitching, called "one pass."

Three-thread serged seams If you have access to a serger, a balanced three-thread overlock stitch is a good choice for strong, stretchy seams on both knits and wovens (see the top photo at right). Because this stitch sews the seam and trims and finishes the cut edges with one pass, it's also a quick method. If your machine offers a choice of widths, the narrow width (using the right or inside needle position) makes an attractive seam or edge finish for sheers. Use the wider width (left or outside needle position) for seams on sturdier fabrics.

Tiny machine zigzags A narrow, short zigzag (0.5mm width, 1.5mm to 2mm length) gives the look and accuracy of a plain seam, but it stretches (see the bottom photo at right). It's a good choice for flexible seams on knits and bias-cut wovens. You can sew this in one pass with seam allowances pressed open, or add a second row of stitching then trim

Stitch choices that work well for strong, stretchy lingerie seams include (from top) a topstitched seam followed by a plain seam, both sewn with a tiny zigzag, and the versatile multiple zigzag stitch that reduces tunneling, which is perfect for many elastic applications and can even be used as a decorative stitch.

tip...

For her delicate silk lingerie, designer Andra Gabrielle often uses a teeny three-thread serged seam sewn in cotton embroidery thread, which presses flat for a smooth seamline. The process is quicker than a French seam and creates less bulk where the seam will be crossed with another decorative detail, such as silk ribbon or machine embroidery.

close to it. For fabrics that ravel, try a wider zigzag for the second pass.

Topstitched seams A two-pass variation of the tiny machine zigzag seam, this is a strong, stretchy seam with a clean-finished look. Besides looking neat, the second row of stitching adds strength and tames the seam allowances. This seam has appeared recently in better ready-to-wear lingerie, highlighting the seamlines on a fitted, stretch-velour camisole and creating an interesting texture. A topstitched seam is easy: It's sewn with a short, narrow zigzag, pressed to one side, and topstitched from the right side with the same small zigzag. On a thick or bulky fabric, trim the lower seam allowance before the second stitching. For straight-grain wovens, you can try the same seam using straight stitching. To sew a topstitched seam:

1 Sew a plain seam, right sides together, using a short, narrow zigzag.

2 Press the seam to one side and zigzag again on top of the seam. Trim close to the second stitching, if desired.

Multiple zigzag stitches If your machine offers this stitch, you'll find that it's handy and versatile for many applications. It functions like a wide zigzag, but the multiple stitches in each "zag" reduce the fabric's tendency to tunnel inside the stitches, as on a regular wide zigzag. Use it when applying elastics, especially clear tape elastic (which tends to fold or curl), or anytime you need to anchor something wide with a stretchy stitch. It also makes a beautiful decorative stitch when lengthened and used as topstitching with single or twin needles and rayon machine-embroidery thread.

Karen's Closet

The camisole at right won its way into my wardrobe because of its interesting seam details, sewn with a zigzag topstitched seam. (The fact that it's sewn from rich red crushed polyester/Lycra velour didn't hurt, either.) With the side seams plus front and back princess seams, this small garment is bisected by six vertical seams, which become vertical design elements and create its curvy shape. The upper edge is bound with a strip of matching fabric, and it has narrow, adjustable straps made of strap elastic. It's an easy garment to copy using tracing paper to trace the shape of each garment section, then adding seam allowances and hems. Or you can start with a pattern in a similar shape, drawing and adding extra seams if needed. Don't forget to label the sections for center front and back and side front and back so you don't get them mixed up.

Comfort Zone

For lingerie that's comfortable and easy to wear, garments need to be finished as smoothly inside as out. One of the places this counts most is at the neckline. For a smooth neckline seam on a simple collar, I prefer to omit the neckline facings (there's nothing worse than a facing that flops out of a gown or robe). Instead of facings, you can cover the collar seam with a narrow band of fabric.

Stitch the collar on first, sewing the seam allowances to the inside or outside, depending on the garment style and where the seam will be less obtrusive (if the collar will be worn open, sew the seam allowances to the outside). Then cover the seam allowances with a 1¼-in.-wide strip of matching or contrasting bias woven or crossgrain knit fabric or with a ½-in.-wide strip of soft cotton twill tape. For the fabric strip, press ⅜ in. under on all four edges of the strip. Center the strip over the seam and pin it in place, then topstitch close to the folded edge around all sides. Your collar join is now smoothly finished, inside and out.

Overlock seams If you don't own a serger, a machine overlock stitch can give the effect of a serged seam with the raw edges enclosed by the stitches. It's quick because it sews and finishes the seam allowances in one pass. Many sewing machines offer a selection of these strong stretch stitches for joining and "serging" seams in knits and Lycra blends, which can be especially useful on camisoles, panties, and swimwear. The stitch patterns that include backward stitches are the strongest but are difficult to rip out, so you may want to baste the seam to check sizing before you stitch it. For a clean finish, trim the seam allowances close to the stitching.

Narrow French seams A narrow French seam is a traditional, fine seam finish for silk lingerie, especially on sheers and fabrics that ravel, because it completely encloses the fabric's raw

Both the French seam (left) and the flat-felled seam (right) completely enclose a seam's raw edges, making them perfect for fabrics that ravel such as silk, linen, and flannel. The French seam lies on the inside of the garment, looking like an ordinary seam from the outside, while the flat-felled seam reveals two rows of stitching from the outside for a sportier look.

Narrow French Seams

A French seam encloses the raw edges of a seam allowance and requires two passes of straight stitching.

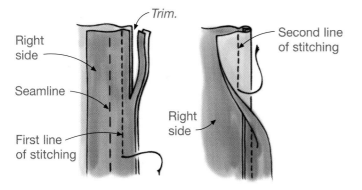

With wrong sides together, stitch ¼ in. from the edge. Trim, press, then fold right sides together and press again. Stitch, enclosing the raw edges.

edges using two passes of stitching (see the photo on p. 37). A French seam can work well on a simple garment with fairly straight lines. However, it may add undesirable stiffness or bulk on a bias-cut garment or on thin fabrics such as chiffon, and it doesn't work well on steep curves. Always test on a sample to be sure you like the result.

To sew a narrow French seam on a ½-in. to ⅝-in. seam allowance (see the illustration above):

1 With wrong sides together, stitch a ¼-in. seam. Press the seam open, then closed. Trim to ⅛ in.

2 Turn the right sides together, and press with the seam on the edge. Stitch ¼ in. from the fold, enclosing the raw edges.

Flat-felled seams When sewing a sporty style in a fabric that ravels easily, such as linen or flannel pajamas, invest a little extra time to create flat-felled seams, which eliminate raw edges inside and out by using two passes of straight stitching. This sturdy seam finish is often seen in ready-to-wear, adding a polished, finished look while accenting the seamlines. It's ideal for medium-to-heavy woven fabrics that ravel, such as linen and many cottons, including cotton flannel. Since a pair of linen pajamas will last nearly forever, you want your seams to last just as long.

To sew a flat-felled seam:

1 Sew the seams wrong sides together using a ⅝-in. seam allowance. Press the seam open, then to one side.

2 Trim the lower seam allowance to ¼ in. and press under the upper seam allowance.

3 From the right side, edgestitch to the garment along the folded edge.

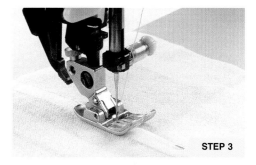

STEP 3

To complete the flat-felled seam, turn under the upper seam allowance and topstitch close to the folded edge.

Decorative Piped Seams

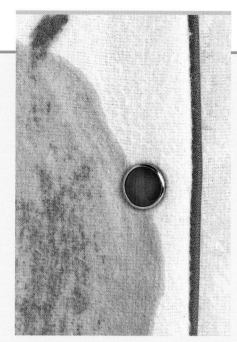

Piping, especially a fine, narrow version sewn in a contrasting color, can add polish as well as strength when used to outline seams and edges of better lingerie and sleepwear. Piping takes a little extra sewing time, since it requires two extra passes of stitching, but the effect is definitely worth it. Piping adds thickness to the seam or edge (how much depends on the thickness of your piping fabric and filler), so although it can be very effective on sturdy fabrics, I don't suggest it for a very thin, fluid garment.

You can create piping from bias-cut strips of woven fabric or crossgrain strips of most knits (cut the strips in the direction of greater stretch). To determine the width of the strips, use twice the width of the seam allowance plus twice the desired width of the finished piping. For example, for ⅝-in. seams and ⅛-in.-wide piping, cut the strips to 1½ in.

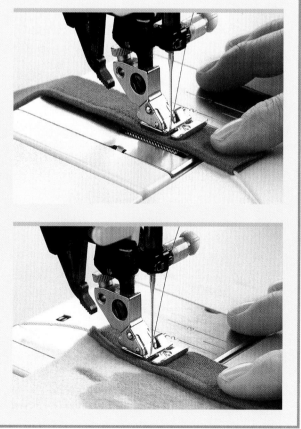

❏ Wrap a piping strip around a skinny filler such as cotton crochet cord or thin yarn. Stitch about 1/16 in. from the cord using a zipper foot (see the center photo at right).

❏ Baste the piping in place on one of the edges to be joined, matching the cut edges and sewing over the previous stitching (see the bottom photo at right), then join the seam as usual. Sew with the basted side on top and stitch 1/16 in. closer to the cord to ensure that the previous lines of stitching won't show in the finished piping. Trim the seam allowances to reduce bulk.

For a delicate, narrow hem on sheer fabrics such as silk chiffon, use a tiny maybelle hem, also known as a narrow turned hem. Only one row of stitching shows from the right side.

Choices for hems and edges

The most attractive finish for each hem and edge will depend on your fabric and whether the garment you're creating is elegant or everyday style. For many innerwear pieces, hems and edges need to be smooth and nearly invisible under clothing. On an elegant garment, you may want a tiny, delicate hem. For pj's and loungewear, you'll probably choose a sturdy, long-lasting hem.

As always, try out the following hem and edge techniques on samples first. The options listed for hems work better on a straight or slightly curved line, while those listed for hems and edges can be applied successfully to curves, such as neck and armhole edges.

Narrow turned hems A tiny, ⅛-in. machine-sewn hem, sometimes called a maybelle hem, is a delicate but strong edge finish for fine fabrics, including sheers like chiffon (see the photo above). Sewn with two passes of straight stitching, this hem makes an easy, attractive finish.

1 Using pins, mark ⅛ in. below the desired hemline.

2 Fold along the pins and straight-stitch close to the fold without stretching, removing pins as you sew. Trim excess fabric close to the stitching.

3 Turn up a ⅛-in. hem and stitch again over the first line of stitching.

Narrow scalloped hems Sewn with one pass of stitching using a rolled hemmer foot, a scalloped hem creates a decorative edge on lightweight synthetic fabrics such as nylon tricot and chiffon (see the top photo on the facing page). Although it's quick to sew and often used in ready-to-wear, it's not as thin or smooth as a turned hem. Before sewing, stretch the fabric edge to see which way it curls, then sew the hem rolled in this direction. On tricot, this means that the hem will be rolled to the right side. Use matching thread and a long, wide zigzag stitch that's nearly as wide as the hem

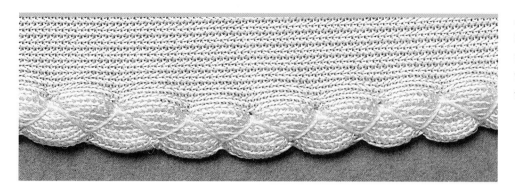

A narrow scalloped hem looks elegant on fabrics like nylon tricot that tend to curl to the right side.

(as determined by the hemmer foot); the stitch draws in the edge, creating the scallop. A longer stitch results in a larger, more dramatic scallop.

1 Sew a few stitches near the edge of the fabric, and use the thread ends to draw fabric into the scroll of the rolled hemmer foot.

2 Stitch the hem using a long zigzag stitch that's just wide enough to draw in the hem edge (see the photo below).

A sturdy turned hem makes a practical finish for pajama pants and other casual garments. Anchor it with a single row of topstitching or with a more decorative stitch, like this twin-needle multiple zigzag sewn in contrasting thread.

A fairly wide, long zigzag stitch creates the scallop, pulling in the rolled edge as it forms inside the rolled hemmer foot.

Sturdy turned hems This durable, double-turned, 1-in. or wider hem makes a clean finish on fabrics such as cotton flannel or linen and requires one pass of stitching (see the photo above). It's perfect for hems on pajama sleeves and pants. To sew a sturdy turned hem:

1 Turn under a 1¼-in.- to 1¾-in.-wide hem, then press under ¼ in. at the raw edge.

2 Topstitch close to the edge with straight stitching.

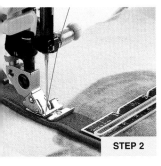
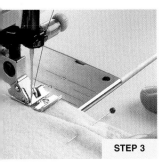
On knits and other fabrics that don't ravel, you can sew a thinner, single-turned hem by omitting the second turn. Topstitching from the right side with a twin needle gives a professional finish.

Fake piped hems It's easy to create a neat piped hem at the lower sleeve of a pajama or robe to complement piping elsewhere on the garment without sewing on a separate band (see the photo below). This finish requires three passes of stitching, plus one to make the piping. Allow 1 in. extra length in the sleeve plus 2½ in. for the sleeve hem to create finished piping that lies 2 in. above the finished sleeve edge.

1 Construct the piping following the instructions for a decorative piped seam given in the sidebar on p. 39.

2 Lay the piping on the sleeve with the stitching line 5½ in. above the cut edge and seam allowances pointing toward the edge. Baste the piping in place, then trim the seam allowances to a scant ½ in.

3 Fold the lower sleeve up over the piping and pin to enclose piping seam allowances, then stitch from the other side, following previous stitching and sewing just inside it.

4 To reduce bulk in heavy fabric such as cotton flannel, trim the layers, then press the seam toward the lower sleeve. Sew the sleeve seam, then

Step 2: To create fake piping, baste the piping onto the flat sleeve.

Step 3: Fold the lower sleeve up over the piping, then stitch from the basted side, sewing just inside the line of basting stitches.

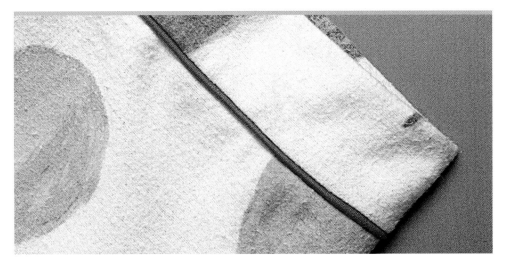

A fake piped hem makes an attractive finish at the lower sleeve of a pj shirt or robe to tie in with piping elsewhere on the garment, without the hassle of adding a separate fabric section.

turn up 2½ in. for the hem, turning under the raw edge. From the right side, hem the sleeve by stitching just above and very close to the piping, using a zipper foot.

Fabric-bound hems or edges A fabric binding makes a beautiful hem or edge finish and can also continue to form the garment's straps (see the photo below). The binding can be any width, but narrower bindings curve more easily to follow a shaped edge. I find a ⅜-in. finished binding to be an attractive and functional width. To bind an edge, use a bias strip of woven fabric or crossgrain strip of knit. Cut the strip's width three times the desired finished measurement of the binding plus ½ in., and cut the

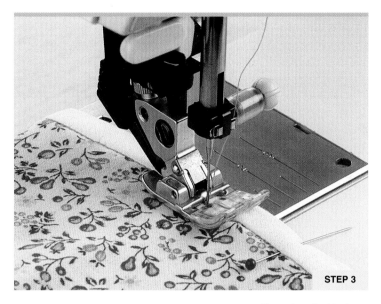

STEP 3

To anchor the binding's inner edge, stitch in the ditch of the seam from the right side.

length slightly shorter than the finished edge (three-quarters to seven-eighths of the edge length typically works well). For an edge that's a closed circle, you'll need to sew the binding in a circle before applying it.

1. With right sides together, place the strip on the edge, matching cut edges, and stitch using a seam allowance the width of the finished binding, stretching the strip slightly.

2. Press and wrap the binding to the inside, turn under the binding's inner edge, and pin in place. Press again.

3. From the right side, stitch in the ditch of the seam to anchor the inner edge of the binding.

To create straps, attach the binding as explained on pp. 54–59. Turn in both long edges so the binding continues at a uniform width, then edgestitch.

A self-fabric binding makes a clean finish at the neck and armhole edges of a nightgown or camisole and can continue to form the garment's straps.

A turned lace hem neatly eliminates raw edges inside and out, making it ideal for fabrics that ravel. For the second pass of stitching, a hand running stitch sewn in 4mm silk ribbon anchors the top edge of the lace.

Serged hems or edges A tiny two- or three-thread rolled hem, if your serger has one, makes a quick, attractive hem or edge finish on delicate fabrics and is completed in one pass. If you're sewing on silk, stitch the hem using fine cotton machine-embroidery thread for a soft, flat edge.

Lace hems or edges For a quick lace finish on a fabric that doesn't ravel, simply lap a strip of stable or stretch lace over the cut edge and stitch close to the lace's inner edge with a tiny zigzag (see the bottom photo on p. 29). Trim any excess fabric behind the lace. If your fabric tends to ravel, zigzag or serge the cut edge before applying the lace, or use a turned lace hem.

tip. . .

If you are adding lace at the neckline of a camisole, you can extend the ends of the lace to form the camisole straps if desired. Sew lace to the center-front section first, then sew the side-front and back sections, leaving extra lace at the side front for the straps.

For a stretchy fabric, choose a stretch lace, which you can use to draw in the edge slightly if needed. This finish works especially well on stretchy Lycra-blend fabrics such as the velour camisole shown in the photo on p. 60.

Turned lace hems or edges This two-pass finish works well when applying lace to an edge that ravels, or anytime you want to eliminate the fabric's raw edge for a smooth finish inside and out. I used this method to apply the narrow cotton lace hem on the yellow seersucker camisole and half-slip shown in the photo above and on p. 14.

1. Place the right side of the lace trim to the wrong side of the garment, matching edges. Without stretching, sew ¼ in. from the edge of the trim using a narrow zigzag.

2. Turn the trim to the right side. Press, trimming the raw edge of the fabric if necessary. Stitch again at the top of the trim, enclosing the fabric's raw edge, or hand-sew with silk ribbon, as explained on p. 131.

Faced lace hems or edges For a smooth, nonitchy hem or edge on a tricot slip or gown using nylon lace, leave a layer of fabric behind the lace to serve as a lining. This finish requires two passes of stitching, one on each long edge of the lace. For a curved edge, choose a flexible lace and gently steam it to shape before applying it to the garment, or cut the lace at intervals along a motif and overlap to form the curve.

tip...

To steam a length of lace into a curve before attaching it to a garment, lay the lace on the ironing board and gently shape it into a curve like that of the garment edge. Without resting the iron on the lace, steam the lace thoroughly, patting it to create a smooth curve. Allow the lace to cool and dry before sewing it to the garment.

1 After sewing garment seams, lay the lace on top of the hem or edge without stretching either layer, right sides up and matching outer edges.

2 Zigzag along all edges of the lace (including cuts that form a curve, if needed). To finish lace in a circle, trim the end of the lace along a motif and pin over the beginning edge. Zigzag along the cut edge of the end.

Ribbon hems Silk ribbon adds an elegant finish at the edge of delicate, special-occasion lingerie, with or without decorative embroidery and beading.

After finishing the cut edge with a serger or by using a maybelle hem (another option is to place the selvage at the edge when cutting out the garment), simply lap a flat ribbon over the fabric

To create a faced lace hem on a nonravely fabric, simply lay the lace over the hem without stretching, and zigzag around the edges of the lace. For a polished finish where the lace overlaps itself (as on a tubular slip), cut the top layer of lace along the motif and zigzag along this line to join the two layers.

For a delicate ribbon hem, lap a strip of ribbon over a finished edge and sew in place along the top edge of the ribbon using a tiny zigzag.

Use lustrous silk ribbon to bind and finish a cut edge of fabric, either on a straight or curved edge. (*Garment by Andra Gabrielle.*)

edge and sew at the top ribbon edge with a tiny zigzag (see the top photo). Another option is to stitch along the center of the ribbon with a multiple zigzag or other decorative stitch and rayon machine-embroidery thread. If desired, hand-sew tiny seed beads at regular intervals using doubled thread and a running stitch.

Silk ribbon-bound edges You can create a narrow, elegant bound neckline or armhole edge on special-occasion lingerie using silk ribbon, which wraps and finishes the cut edge (see the photo at left). It requires 7mm-wide ribbon, two passes of stitching, and a light touch.

1 On the wrong side, pin the ribbon to the cut edge, matching edges and taking care not to stretch or distort the edge. Sew along the ribbon's inner edge with a 2mm straight stitch, then trim the seam allowance in half.

2 Fold the ribbon over the edge to the right side, and anchor the edge with a tiny zigzag stitch, allowing only the right swing of the stitch to catch the ribbon.

Elastic

If you take a look at the lingerie in your own collection, you'll find that elastic is a key ingredient in numerous types of lingerie. In fact, elastic is what makes many lingerie garments function. It's the

Banish the Bumps

Ready-to-wear panties can leave uncomfortable dents in your skin thanks to the way the elastic is joined. Those big, serged lumps of elastic on the leg openings (and sometimes at the waist, too) are caused by a quick construction method that applies the leg elastic first, then joins the side seams and the elastic at once. It doesn't take long to sew these details the right way, but the extra couple of minutes is just too expensive for manufacturers who try to keep their costs to a minimum. Home sewers can do better, and the superior results are worth the small amount of extra effort. Avoiding this problem is a simple matter of applying leg and waist elastics in a circle after the side seams are sewn.

To make panty legs and waists even smoother, create a neat, flat seam where you join the elastic in a circle. Place the join near a side seam, far away from the crotch area. If you're joining a fairly thin type of elastic, lap the ends ½ in. and stitch to secure it.

For easier stitching on slippery clear elastic, overlap the ends and pin them to a small piece of plain paper, zigzag through the elastic and paper, then tear away the paper (see the top elastic in the photo below). If the doubled elastic seems too thick, as cotton/rubber swimwear elastic tends to be, try butting the ends of the elastic and pinning them to a scrap of thin, stable fabric (like a scrap of thin Lycra knit) or to a scrap of ribbon or twill tape. Use a wide plain or multiple zigzag to join the butted ends, then trim away the

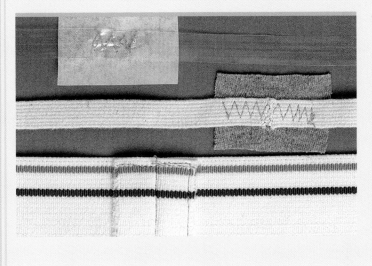

excess fabric (see the center elastic at left).

For wider elastic that will be exposed (such as men's underwear elastic), place the elastic right sides together and sew in a regular ⅝-in. seam. Fold the seam open, stitch around the square in a neat box, and trim the ends close to the stitching (see the bottom elastic at left). I like to place this neat-looking join at the center back as it is on many ready-to-wear garments.

essential edge finish on bras and panties, at the waist of half-slips and pj pants, and on many other garments as well.

In order for elastic to draw in a garment's edge, you'll always cut the elastic shorter than the garment opening; how much shorter depends on the garment style, the application method, and the type of elastic you're using. For some applications, such as a sewn casing, you can wait to try on the garment before adjusting the elastic's final length. For other applications in which the elastic will be cut first, some patterns suggest the elastic measurements for each size.

In general, I suggest cutting the elastic length to 75 percent to 85 percent of the garment opening. Since lingerie elastic and stretch lace are softer and stretchier than most regular elastics, you can cut them using the shorter suggested measurement. If you're not sure, test by wrapping the elastic around your body to see what feels comfortable, and remember that stitching on the elastic will loosen it a bit. If needed, always feel free to adjust the elastic length so it's comfortable for your body.

If you're making garments from quality fabrics that you plan to wear and enjoy for a long time, it makes sense to spend a few extra minutes on the techniques that will set your garment apart from the ordinary. By intelligently choosing not only which elastic but also which elastic application to use for each situation, you can ensure the best results and longest life for every garment you sew.

Be sure to choose an elastic and an application method that suit your taste, your fabric, your garment style, and the amount of time you want to spend

Comfort Zone

Do you own a panty that rides up in back, so you have to keep backing into a corner all day to discretely tug it down? If you do, it's not likely that it gets much wear. Sewing your own lingerie offers a solution, a way to apply panty elastic to correct this problem. The secret lies in how you distribute the gathers of excess fabric along the elastic: by placing more of it in the back.

Many instruction sheets direct you to divide the panty leg and elastic evenly in quarters, marking with pins or dots, and matching the marks during stitching. That's where the problem comes in. Instead, apply the elastic on leg openings unevenly. There should be little easing or gathers at the front of the leg, and the bulk of the fullness should be placed at the lower-back area of the leg. This allows enough fabric in back to cup under your curves and stay there all day.

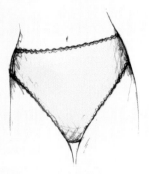

While shopping to research shapes for this book, I discovered a rare find—a comfortable, name-brand panty with the perfect shape and cut for my body, as shown at right. I was excited about my discovery, but by the second washing, the exposed, lapped elastic began to unravel at one of the leg openings. Next, the loosely knitted cotton fabric formed a hole that needed mending. This was obviously a "disposable" garment, not a keeper. This panty became a good model for my shape experiments—but certainly not an enduring part of my wardrobe or an economical purchase.

If you've never splurged and bought yourself a $15 to $20 European cotton panty (on sale is good!), they're definitely worth the price. Made from the finest silky, tightly knitted cotton, these panties normally leave no exposed elastic to touch your skin, and they last for years. Although it takes a few extra minutes to cover the elastic on the panties you sew, at least experiment on a pair to decide if the added comfort and durability are worth the extra effort for you. Whenever I sew a panty, this quality is what I aim for, and it performs as well as the top-quality European panties I've bought in the past.

sewing. In chapter 2, I discussed some of the different types of elastic; here you'll find a variety of elastic applications. Try making a sample of each to decide which is most comfortable for you; these samples will help you make the best decisions for each garment.

Turned and covered elastic

Turned and covered elastic is my preferred method for most elastic applications. It takes a little longer to sew, but covered elastic feels better on the skin and results in a more durable garment. It also eliminates the problem of finding lingerie elastic to match or coordinate with each fabric because it requires only regular elastic, which won't show in the finished garment. My favorite choice for

a comfortable turned edge on panty leg openings is clear polyurethane elastic because it is thin, stretchy, and resilient. At the waist, I prefer a wider-than-usual elastic like 1¼-in.-wide men's underwear elastic.

A covered-elastic application works best on thin, smooth fabrics. Since it results in two layers of fabric plus a layer of elastic, it may be too bulky on a thicker fabric. In this case, it may be better to use softer lingerie elastic and the "turned, uncovered elastic" method on pp. 53–54, which neatly covers the cut edge but leaves the elastic exposed. Another option is to add a thinner, contrast binding with elastic, noted on pp. 51–52.

A turned elastic application usually involves adding a seam allowance to most panty patterns. Read the pattern to see which elastic application it suggests. If it shows a lapped elastic application, you'll need to add seam allowances. Add the width of the elastic you'll use at that opening, typically ½ in. to 1¼ in. at the waist and ⅜ in. at the leg.

1 Join the cut edges of elastic in a circle, using one of the methods discussed in the sidebar on p. 47.

2 For a waist opening, mark the elastic loop and opening in quarters, placing the join at a side seam. For a leg opening, you have a choice: Either mark and apply the elastic in quarters evenly, or disregard the marks and place more of the excess fabric at the lower-back leg area.

3 Place the elastic on the wrong side of the cut edge, matching edges, and sew with a narrow zigzag along the outer edge of the elastic. For slippery, clear elastic, sew down the center with a wide multiple zigzag, if you have one, or with a wide normal zigzag.

4 Turn the elastic to the inside. For a professional-looking finish, topstitch from the right side using a narrow twin needle (size 1.6/70) so that you catch the cut edge. Or stitch again along the inner edge using a narrow zigzag or down the center using a wide multiple zigzag, depending on the look you prefer.

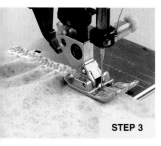

STEP 3

STEP 4

Step 3: With the elastic on the wrong side of the fabric and matching edges, use a multiple zigzag down the center, stretching the elastic to fit.

Step 4: Turn the elastic to the inside and topstitch from the right side using a narrow twin needle, stretching slightly and catching the cut edge of the fabric in the stitching.

tip. . .

For a slight tummy-controlling effect, use wider-than-usual 1¼-in. elastic at the waist edge of your panties. Add a seam allowance the same width as the elastic, and apply it using a turned application so the elastic is completely enclosed, creating a smooth, covered finish. Topstitch from the right side using a narrow twin needle.

Sewn casing with inserted elastic

Another polished, covered-elastic finish is a stitched casing with the elastic threaded through it, as seen at the waist of better slips and on fine-quality panties from the Swiss company Calida. Sewn in only one pass, a casing has another advantage: You can try on and adjust the length of the elastic after you insert it, and you can easily replace the elastic if it wears out before the garment (which is often the case).

For this finish, add a seam allowance the width of the elastic plus ½ in. for ease and for turning under the raw edge. On a stable knit that doesn't ravel, it's not necessary to turn under the raw edge, especially if you'll be topstitching the casing with a narrow twin needle. In this case, add the width of the elastic plus ¼ in. for ease. To make a sewn casing with inserted elastic:

1 Turn the seam allowance to the inside, turning under the raw edge ¼ in. if desired. Press, then stitch close to the lower fold or topstitch from the right side using a narrow twin needle, leaving a small opening

Comfort Zone

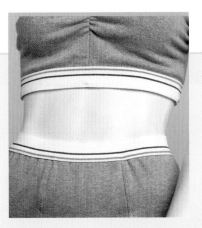

Striped men's underwear elastic isn't just for men. It can also be used decoratively on a sports bra, exposed for a sportier look and "lined" with soft cotton knit bra-lining fabric for extra comfort, if desired.

To line the elastic with fabric, apply it to the edge using a reverse variation of the "turned, uncovered elastic" application discussed on pp. 53–54, which gives a cushioned finish with no raw edges. After joining the elastic in a circle, place the elastic and garment wrong sides together, lapping the elastic just ¼ in. over the cut edge. Sew ⅛ in. from the edge of the elastic using a medium zigzag stitch. Turn the elastic to the right side, and zigzag again at the top edge. The result is a fashionable look with a very comfortable feel.

to insert the elastic. If you'd like a crisp edge at the waist, stitch again close to the top edge of the casing.

2 Thread the elastic through the casing using a long safety pin or a large, blunt needle, and overlap the ends. Try it on to adjust the length, then stitch the ends securely.

3 To prevent the elastic from twisting, adjust the gathers evenly and top-stitch through the elastic along the seamlines and at the center front and center back.

Contrast binding with elastic

This more elaborate covered-elastic application is one you may not use often on lingerie, but it's a good technique to know about. Requiring three passes of stitching, a contrast binding can add a band of decorative color and neatly enclose the elastic at an edge (see

A neat casing encloses the elastic, making a smooth waist on a half-slip. To create a crisp finish at the top, edgestitch along the fold. For a polished hem at the casing's lower edge, sew from the right side using a narrow twin needle.

A contrast binding with elastic allows you to add another color to your garment while minimizing bulk at the edge.

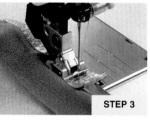

STEP 3

STEP 4

Step 3: Place elastic over the binding, and sew using a long, wide zigzag, stretching the elastic to fit.

Step 4: Wrap the binding to the right side, turning under the raw edge so the fold just covers the basting, and pin. Stitch from the right side with a wide twin needle.

the photo above). Although it's typically seen on beautiful swimwear, this technique makes sense for lingerie if you're sewing a panty from a heavier-weight fabric but want to add covered elastic at the openings. This method allows you to create a thinner edge by cutting the binding from a coordinating, lightweight fabric. The binding eliminates the need for an added seam allowance at the edge.

1 From binding fabric, cut strips four times the width of the elastic (1½ in. for ⅜-in. elastic) in the direction of greater stretch. Cut the binding strip length to 90 percent of the opening edge, and sew the ends to close the loop, if you're applying the binding to a closed circle. Mark the binding and edge in quarters with pins.

2 Baste the right side of the binding to the wrong side of the garment, matching raw edges and marks and stretching the binding to fit. If needed to reduce bulk, trim the binding close to the basting.

3 Apply the elastic over the binding seam, aligning edges, using a long, wide zigzag and stretching the elastic to fit.

4 Fold the binding to the right side, turning the raw edge under so the fold just covers the basting stitches, and pin. Topstitch from the right side using a twin needle (size 4.0/75), stretching the binding evenly.

Quick lapped elastic or stretch lace

Lapped elastic can be applied in a quick, one-pass method that's frequently seen on ready-to-wear lingerie and suggested in many lingerie patterns. This fast, inexpensive technique works well for stretch lace, however, it's not my method of choice for most other applications.

There's no need to add a seam allowance at the garment opening when using this technique.

1 Cut the elastic to length as suggested in your pattern (about 75 percent of the opening), and sew the elastic in a circle.

2 For a waist opening, mark the elastic and opening edge in quarters with pins. Lap the elastic over the cut edge of the fabric, right sides up. For a leg opening, either mark it in quarters or place more of the excess fabric at the lower-back leg (see p. 48).

3 Sew along the inner edge of the elastic with a narrow zigzag, matching the marks. Trim excess fabric on the wrong side.

Covering the Exposed Join in Lapped Elastic

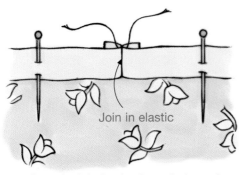

1. Sew the join in elastic and pin to the edge.

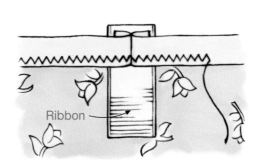

2. Insert a 2-in. to 3-in. piece of ½-in. ribbon under the elastic, then sew the elastic to the edge.

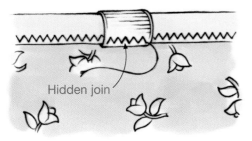

3. Fold the ribbon around to the back and bar-tack or stitch in the ditch to secure.

For a neater join in exposed elastic, smoothly cover the join with a piece of satin ribbon, as shown in the illustration above. You can also use a strip of tricot or self-fabric, turning in the raw edges before sewing it into the seam.

Turned, uncovered elastic

If you're using lingerie elastic, this modified turned edge gives a nice finish with no exposed raw edges of fabric. This method, which requires two passes of stitching, places the elastic on the inside of the garment and allows the delicate picot edge to show from the outside.

When cutting out the garment, add a seam allowance to the edge that is the same width as the elastic.

1 Lay the elastic on the garment with right sides up, matching edges, with the picot edge facing toward the garment (see the top photo on p. 54). Using a tiny zigzag, sew along the elastic's inner edge, just inside the picot, matching marks and stretching the elastic to fit. Trim excess fabric behind the elastic.

2 Turn the elastic to the inside, then stitch again along the inner edge (see the bottom left photo on p. 54).

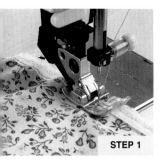

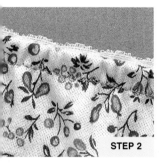

Step 1: Lay the elastic on the right side of the fabric, matching edges, with the picot edge facing into the garment. Zigzag along the elastic's inner edge, just inside the picot, stretching the elastic to fit. Trim the excess fabric under the elastic.

Step 2: Turn the elastic to the inside and sew again along the inner edge.

Fold-over elastic edges A fold-over elastic edge appears on many current ready-to-wear lingerie garments, especially on stretchy, snug-fitting camisoles, where the elastic binds the edge and forms the straps in a continuous piece (see the photo below). It gives a quick, professional-looking finish with one pass of stitching and is a good choice if you don't mind elastic touching your skin. Purchase ½-in.-wide satiny elastic with a foldline at the center (these are often available in white and black in ½-in. and 1-in. widths, which finish to half of that).

To make a camisole with a fold-over elastic edge and straps:

1 Apply elastic to the camisole's center-front section. Fold the elastic to enclose the cut edge, and sew through all layers with a narrow zigzag along the inner edge of the elastic, stretching the elastic slightly to pull in the edge.

2 Cut a piece of elastic long enough to bind the back and sides and to form two straps. Fold and edgestitch one strap-length of the elastic, then insert one side-front edge into the elastic, encasing the cut end of the front elastic, as shown in the photo in the facing page. Stitch around the camisole to the other side front.

3 Continue edgestitching on the folded elastic to create the second strap. Anchor straps to the camisole back as described on the facing page.

Straps

There are many interesting strap options for a lingerie garment. In my opinion, delicate spaghetti and twisted silk-ribbon straps look beautiful on a nightgown or special-occasion garment, but they tend to slip and don't provide much support.

For everyday wear, I prefer straps of narrow strap elastic or stretch lace,

Quickly finish the edge of a camisole or slip with a neat strip of fold-over elastic, which strengthens and binds the raw edge with one pass of stitching.

After sewing along the folded elastic to form a strap, insert the side-front edge of the camisole into the fold-over elastic and continue stitching around the camisole, stretching the elastic slightly.

which are very easy to make. Another comfortable style is a camisole in which the fabric that wraps over the shoulder is a narrow extension of the garment fabric, technically not a strap at all (like the one shown on p. 24). The following are several popular strap options, with general instructions on how to attach them to the garment.

Attaching straps securely

Before sewing the second end of a non-adjustable strap to your garment, be sure to pin it in place and try on the garment for final adjustments. If straps tend to slip off your shoulders, attach straps closer to the center back. The strap attachment will be stronger if you stitch it twice.

To attach the end of a strap to a garment:

1 On the inside, place the strap on the garment with the raw end facing up toward the garment edge. Stitch across the strap ½ in. or more from the end, hiding your stitches in the ditch of a lace, elastic, or bound edge if possible. Trim the end.

2 Fold the strap up to cover the cut end, then stitch again securely. If the garment has a lace edge, stitch once on the garment fabric and once on the lace to prevent excess stress on the lace.

Purchased lingerie straps

Lingerie suppliers and fabric stores sell adjustable straps that are ready to sew into your garments. Made from strap elastic with adjusting hardware, they're typically available in white, black, and beige only, although the white ones can be dyed with your garment, as discussed on pp. 112–115.

Adjustable straps from strap elastic

Lingerie suppliers also sell strap elastic by the yard in the same basic colors. To make the straps adjustable, purchase a pair each of strap rings and slide adjusters to fit your elastic width (both are available in various sizes in painted metal or clear plastic). I prefer skinny ¼-in. strap elastic when I can find it, otherwise ⅜ in. will do (for more support, ⅝-in. width is also available). On some styles, like many bras, you'll place the ring and adjuster at the garment front. On other styles, like some camisoles, the ring and adjuster fall at the back.

tip. . .

Remember that straps don't always have to be adjustable when a garment is custom-made. Manufacturers use adjustable straps so their garments will fit as many bodies as possible. But if you like the look of lingerie hardware or find yourself adjusting your straps due to weight fluctuations or monthly variations, by all means include adjusters on your straps.

BRINGING CLOSURE TO YOUR LINGERIE

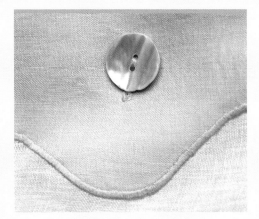

When selecting a button for sleepwear, think about whether you'd be comfortable lying on it or not.

W hen it comes to selecting a closure for your lingerie garments, anything goes! The same wide range of options from your everyday wardrobe are also available for lingerie. Depending on the garment, you might plan a closure that adds a design detail, such as a vertical row of tiny, hand-sewn hooks and eyes for a snug, cotton/Lycra camisole, or something more simple and functional, such as standard buttons or snaps. Whatever you choose, remember to match the closure to the task. Large, lumpy buttons or stiff zippers on sleepwear might keep you from getting a good, comfortable night's sleep.

Buttons

The right button can add an interesting element to your lingerie, but make sure the size and style suit the garment. For innerwear, choose a small, flat button that won't show under clothing. On sleepwear, you still want something flat and comfortable, like the natural pearl buttons on my white linen pajama shown in the top photo at right. Or make covered buttons to match or coordinate with your fabric, possibly embellished with machine embroidery before covering. Aside from comfort considerations, let buttons be a part of your embellishment.

An invisible zipper makes a clean closure on a loungewear garment like a furry cotton chenille robe.

Zippers

In my opinion, zippers, at least the ones made with current technologies, are too stiff for sleepwear. But I love the look of an invisible zipper on a robe, like the blue/white summer robe shown below, and zippers can make great closures for loungewear. For an invisible zipper, choose one made by Coats; they're thinner than others on the market.

When inserting an invisible zipper in a pile fabric such as chenille, don't stitch as close to the coil as the instruc-

tions indicate. Leave about ⅛ in. for the pile, or you'll have trouble closing the finished zipper. On a conventional zipper, a purchased or handmade tassel looks great on the pull and makes it easy to grab.

Snaps

I love snaps! Snaps are one way to add a little instant polish to a garment. They're also small, flat, and comfortable on many types of lingerie and work just about anywhere you'd use a button. And no buttonholes to make! If you're applying snaps on thick fabric, make sure your snaps' prongs are long enough to penetrate the layers. Snaps are available in fun colors and designs, and there are several kinds of snap-setting tools to make the task easier.

Hooks and Eyes

Use hooks and eyes on lingerie wherever you want a flat, smooth closure that's also strong. Besides bra-back closures, a series of hooks also can become a decorative element, adding a

certain vintage look. Individual hooks and eyes require hand-sewing, but you can also purchase hook-and-eye tape that's easy to stitch onto a garment.

Hook-and-Loop Tape

Hook-and-loop tape, commonly known under the brand name Velcro, may not be the first lingerie closure that comes to mind, but don't rule it out. It's a functional option for many loungewear garments, and as the technology for this closure continues to advance, hook-and-loop tape will become even thinner and softer. For now, try Velcro or softer Fixx Velour at the neck of a robe or at the fly-front of loungewear pants.

Ties

A pair of ties can make a soft, comfortable closure at the neck of a robe or peignoir. Sew a pair of quick turned-tube ties from a bias strip of fabric using the spaghetti straps instructions on pp. 58–59. Stitch across one end of the tube to create a closed tie end, or hand-sew the end into a wrapped loop or add a button to give weight at the end. Another beautiful tie design for a delicate, special-occasion garment can be easily made from twisted silk ribbon, with or without a crystal drop at each tie end. You'll find instructions for this tie on pp. 131–132.

Bra Closures

I'll talk more about both hook-and-eye bra-back closures and bra-front closures in chapter 5.

Snaps can add fun dots of color on casual lingerie, and they're relatively small and comfortable for both lounging and sleeping.

To assemble and apply the strap:

1. Wrap the end of a piece of strap elastic around the center bar of the slide adjuster, wrong sides together, and sew securely using a short, narrow zigzag or satin stitch (see the illustration below).

2. Thread the other end of the strap through the ring, then insert the end through the slide.

3. Stitch the cut end of the strap securely to the garment front or back, as explained on p. 55.

4. To attach the ring end, cut a 1-in. to 1½-in. piece of elastic, fold it over the ring, and stitch. Sew it securely to the back or front of the garment as desired.

Assembling an Adjustable Strap

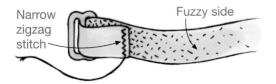

Narrow zigzag stitch

Fuzzy side

Wrap the end of the strap elastic around the center bar of the slide adjuster, wrong (fuzzy) sides together, then sew securely using a short, narrow zigzag stitch.

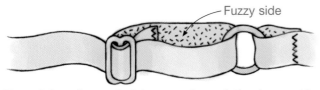

Fuzzy side

Thread the other end of the strap through the ring, and insert the end through the slide.

Straps of stretch lace, fabric binding, or fold-over elastic

Stretch lace straps are an easy style to make. Basically just a strip of lace that's sewn to the garment, the straps can be cut separately and sewn in place or can be created as an extension of the lace edging for the neckline, as described for the fold-over elastic strap and for the bound neckline edge that extends into a strap. After trying on the garment and adjusting the strap length, attach the back end of the strap using the directions on p. 55 or add a ring and slide to make the other back of the strap adjustable.

Wide or skinny turned tubes

Bias tubular straps can be sewn in any width you prefer. In general, the narrower the strap, the more elegant it will look; wider straps tend to be sportier. To make skinny spaghetti straps:

1. Cut bias strips 1 in. wide.

2. Fold the right sides together, then stretch while stitching down the center.

3. Turn the tube. A Fasturn tool makes turning easier, especially on a thin tube, and allows you to open the seam allowances for a smooth strap.

4. Pin the tube to your ironing board, then stretch, steam, and press it to remove as much stretch as possible. Repeat the process so the strap won't continue to stretch when you wear it. Allow the tubes to cool and dry before unpinning.

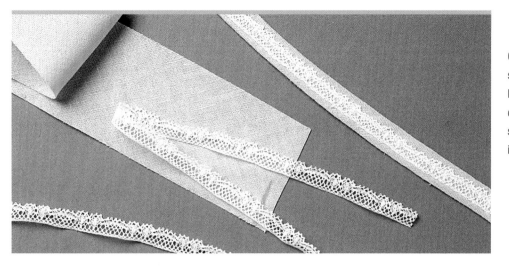

Create an embellished strap by stitching a length of narrow lace or ribbon to a bias strip before sewing it into a tube.

5 Attach one end of each strap as described on p. 55. Try on the garment and pin the straps to the correct length, then sew the other end in place using the same method.

Combination straps with lace or ribbon over fabric

It's easy to make an embellished strap that combines either coordinating ribbon or narrow lace with your garment fabric. Sew the trim to the bias woven or crossgrain strip before you stitch it into a tube.

To create a self-fabric strap embellished with lace or ribbon:

1 Start by cutting bias or crossgrain strips for a wider turned tube strap. Place the trim on your fabric, and measure to determine the ideal width; you'll want some fabric to show on either side of the trim. For a ½-in.-wide finished strap, start with a 2-in.-wide strip.

2 Center a length of narrow lace or ribbon on the strip, and stitch it in place along each long edge.

3 Sew, turn, and steam the tube as described for spaghetti straps, placing the seam at the center back.

Now that you're armed with an arsenal of lingerie-sewing techniques, complete and label your samples for the seams, edge finishes, elastic applications, straps, and closures that interest you. Next, fitting a pattern or creating your own easy pattern will be the final step before you're ready to begin an actual garment.

For a sporty look, make a ⅜-in.-wide self-fabric strap, cutting strips 1½ in. wide on the bias, for a woven. After turning the tube, topstitch along each edge.

FITTING AND CREATING PATTERNS

4

Fitting the human body is probably the single greatest sewing challenge—it often keeps sewers from creating the number and variety of garments that they'd like. But when it comes to fitting, you can relax when sewing most types of lingerie. Lingerie doesn't present nearly as many of the fitting headaches that slow you down when constructing a "serious" garment, like a jacket or pants.

Whether you start with a commercial pattern, make a pattern from a garment you love, or draft your own custom pattern using the instructions in this chapter, there's a certain amount of tinkering involved to get the garment to look and fit the way you want. But thanks to simple shapes, lingerie fabrics that stretch, and a lot of built-in roominess in many cases, fitting is simply less of an issue with lingerie. I'll also include instructions on how to construct a half-slip, camisole, and panty from the custom patterns you make.

Even though innerwear requires a close fit, pieces like this underwire bra and thong still offer pure comfort, since they're sewn from soft, flexible cotton knit with stretchy elastic at all the edges.

Garment Style Determines Fit

Getting a pattern to fit the way you want is one of the keys to success for any garment. Luckily, many types of lingerie are very easy to fit, particularly loungewear and sleepwear. Most garments in the loungewear and sleepwear categories are either stretchy or relaxed and roomy enough to be deliciously comfortable and hassle-free, and the patterns tend to have few pattern pieces and simple, fail-proof shapes. So when I talk about fitting lingerie, sleepwear and loungewear have different requirements than other, more fitted types of lingerie.

Innerwear, on the other hand, does need to be fairly fitted and smooth but still comfortable. For this reason, it makes sense to use a lot of knits and Lycra-blend fabrics, which, with their built-in stretch and recovery, take much of the hassle and stress out of fitting. Even a small amount of stretch in the fabric makes a snug garment so much easier to fit and forgives small errors. If

tip. . .

If your slip doesn't have a wrap opening or slit at the hem, try cutting it in a slight A-line shape, or wider at the hem, for ease when walking and sitting. This is especially helpful if the slip is a longer length.

you're working with wovens, you can get a similar effect by cutting the fabric on the bias for a close, smooth fit that's still flexible and comfortable to wear.

Slips, although innerwear, fall somewhere between these two extremes. By design, they are easy to fit. A half-slip is really just a tube, and most full-slips are tubes with adjustable straps.

Panties, however, are a little more complex because of the body's three-dimensional shape. Lay a pair of panties on your bed and take a look at the shape: They're fuller in the back, and the leg openings lie on the front of the garment. Fitting a panty pattern starts with choosing a style you like, and a number of interesting pattern options are available (see the illustration at left). Since each woman's preference for panty shape is highly individual, I suggest you use a favorite existing pair of panties as a reference to help you make essential decisions about the perfect style and waist height and the ideal shape and height of the leg openings.

Another great way to get exactly the panties you want is to draft your own panty pattern. While this may sound difficult, it truly isn't. Using just four body measurements—waist, hip, waist to hip, and crotch depth—you can quickly draw a basic panty pattern that's

Basic Panty Styles

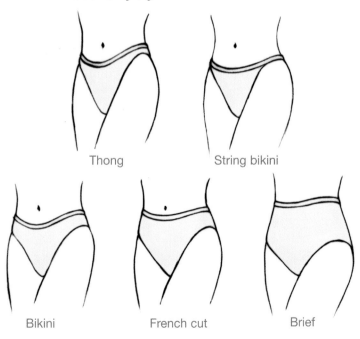

Thong

String bikini

Bikini

French cut

Brief

Measuring Your Body

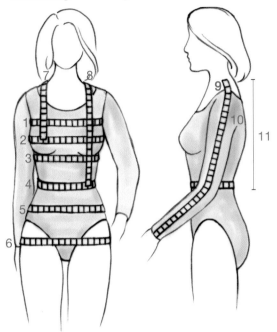

1. High bust (directly under arms)
2. Bust (fullest level)
3. Under bust (ribcage)
4. Waist
5. High hip
6. Hip (fullest level, and note distance from waist)
7. Shoulder to bust point
8. Shoulder to waist
9. Shoulder (width)
10. Sleeve length (shoulder to wrist, with arm bent)
11. Back waist length

custom-fitted to your body. Once you have this paper pattern, it's easy to adjust and customize the shape to develop the type of leg curve and waist height you want.

Bras, another type of innerwear, require the most fitting. Cup fit is very important, since the vast majority of women are wearing bra cups that are too small! After the cup is correct, getting the band to fit is a relatively easy adjustment. And fitting a bra becomes much easier when you use a fabric with at least some stretch. I'll address more of the unique fitting aspects of bras in chapter 5.

Good Fit Starts with Accurate Measuring

The first step in making any type of lingerie, whether you're working with a commercial pattern or creating your own, is to take accurate body measurements. It's best to have someone else help take your measurements, although it's not always easy to round up a helper when you need one. To measure for innerwear, wear undergarments that fit well; if you're sewing sleepwear, this isn't really necessary. You won't need to compare all these measurements every time you sew; just use the ones that relate to the garment you're making and to your figure variations.

First, place a 1-in.-wide belt or pin a piece of firm, nonstretchy ribbon or trim snugly around your waist and adjust it to your natural waistline. This will serve as a guide when taking your waist measurement and front- and back-waist lengths. Especially if you're working alone, stand in front of a full-length mirror so you can check that the tape is level for each measurement.

Measuring Your Full Torso for a Bodysuit or Teddy

Compare your full-torso measurement to that of your pattern to decide whether the pattern needs adjusting.

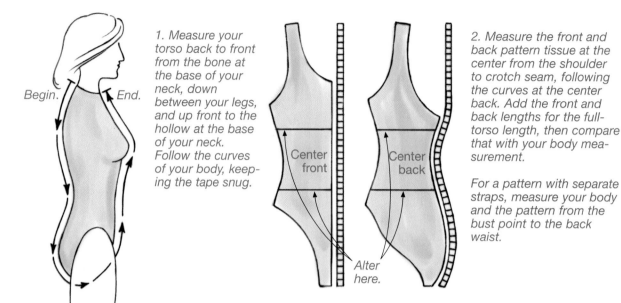

1. Measure your torso back to front from the bone at the base of your neck, down between your legs, and up front to the hollow at the base of your neck. Follow the curves of your body, keeping the tape snug.

Begin. End.

Center front

Center back

Alter here.

2. Measure the front and back pattern tissue at the center from the shoulder to crotch seam, following the curves at the center back. Add the front and back lengths for the full-torso length, then compare that with your body measurement.

For a pattern with separate straps, measure your body and the pattern from the bust point to the back waist.

3. If you need to alter the pattern, adjust the front and back between the bust and waist and/or between the waist and hip.

The illustration on p. 63 lists the body measurements you'll need to know for sewing various types of lingerie. Take your measurements as shown and record them on a sheet of paper. The full-torso measurement, shown in the illustration above, is helpful for fitting one-piece garments like bodysuits and teddies (and also, by the way, for swimsuits). The crotch-depth measurement, shown in the illustration on the facing page, will be used for adjusting pants and for creating a custom panty pattern.

Working with Commercial Patterns

Comparing your body measurements to the suggested measurements on the pattern will, ideally, help you select a pattern size. But many bodies require different sizes in different areas, which can make choosing a pattern size more confusing.

For lingerie other than bras, there's no need to make this complicated. For full-body garments, it's often better to choose a pattern based on your high-

tip. . .

Write down your measurements and date the list for future reference. It's best to measure yourself every six months to a year, since your body may change frequently.

Measuring Crotch Depth

Sit on a flat surface such as a table or countertop. Measure at the side of your body from the bottom of the waistband, over your hip, then straight down to the flat surface. This is your crotch depth.

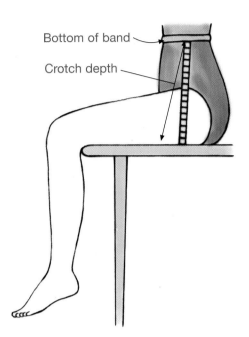

Bottom of band

Crotch depth

bust instead of your bust measurement, especially if your body is larger than your frame or bone structure or if you once used a smaller-size pattern but have gained weight. This will give you a smaller pattern that fits more nicely through the neck and shoulders (the areas that are more difficult to alter and where most women don't gain much weight), and you can easily add width at the bust, waist, and hip for the correct body measurement, including plenty of ease. How much ease depends on your fabric and the kind of fit you want.

Starting with a smaller pattern than your bust measurement indicates will

Comfort Zone

Ease is the difference between the measurement of your body and the measurement of the pattern or garment in a given area. There are really two types of ease: ease that's added for comfort and wearability, and "design ease," which is ease that's added by the designer to create a style or look.

On the back of a pattern envelope, the words used to describe the garment provide a clue as to how much ease the style includes. Words like "fitted" and "close fitting" indicate that less ease is added, while "loose fitting" or "very loose fitting" suggest that the style includes more ease. In general, fluid fabrics require more ease to look and feel right, and firmer fabrics and those that stretch require less. By comparing your body measurement with that of the pattern (after subtracting seam allowances), you'll get an idea of how much ease you will have in an area so you can add more if needed when cutting out the pattern.

Sleepwear and loungewear are generally designed to include plenty of extra ease for comfort so the garment will feel wonderfully unrestricting. Even elegant silk satin and chiffon gowns and robes allow 10 in. or more of ease at the hip. True luxury can also be comfortable! Be sure to check the crotch depth on pajama pants and shorts; I like it to be 1 in. or so deeper than for regular pants. If you don't have plenty of ease, add more. One easy way to check is to compare the crotch depth with that of a pj pant you love.

Innerwear garments generally include a minimal amount of ease so they'll be smooth and bulk-free under outer garments. This is why knits and other stretchy fabrics make so much sense for innerwear—the garment can be sleek and close fitting, even cut smaller than the body, and still be comfortable and easy to fit and wear.

Adjusting a Full-Slip Pattern for a Larger Cup Size

If you're larger than a B cup and want to make a full-slip that fits smoothly in the bust area, a pattern with princess seams is fairly easy to adjust by increasing the curve in the bust area. Tape the side-front pattern over a piece of paper, and redraw the princess-line curves in the bust area to add about ⅜ in. for each cup size above B, tapering to the original seamline above and below the bust apex.

On the center-front pattern, draw a horizontal line at the bust point, cut along the line, and spread the pattern the same amount you added to the side front, taping the pattern to paper. Baste the slip together, then try it on wrong side out so you can adjust the bust area if needed before completing the slip.

Adjusting a Princess-Seam Slip Pattern for a Larger Bust

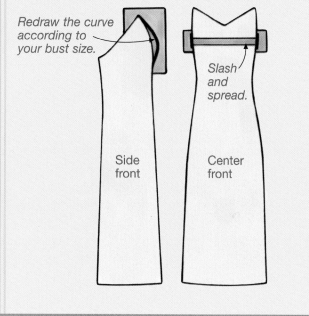

Redraw the curve according to your bust size.

Slash and spread.

Side front

Center front

reduce the chance of having pajamas and gowns with gaping neck openings and baggy shoulders, when what you may really need is just extra room in the bust or hip. For a lower-body garment such as a half-slip, panty, or pair of pants, choose the pattern based on your hip measurement.

If the pattern you choose is multi-sized, with several sizes drawn on each pattern section, then your work becomes easier. Just outline a smaller size to cut the neckline, shoulders, and armholes, and a larger size for the bust and hip to suit your measurements.

Taking fabric stretch into account

When sewing with knits and Lycra-blend fabrics, it's essential to pay attention to the amount of stretch in your fabric. The amount of stretch varies widely between fabrics, from less than 25 percent to 100 percent, and this variation can dramatically affect the fit of your garment. For example, if you're working with a stretchy Lycra-blend fabric, the additional stretch means that the garment can be cut smaller, often even smaller than your body, depending on how you want the garment to fit. Think of a swimsuit: When you hold it up to your body before putting it on, it's definitely smaller than you are.

Patterns designed for stretch fabrics are created with this stretch factor in mind; the back of the pattern envelope will recommend fabrics and tell you the amount of stretch the designer calculated for that style. Because the stretch dramatically affects the fit, it's best to stick with a fabric that has the recommended amount of stretch, at least until

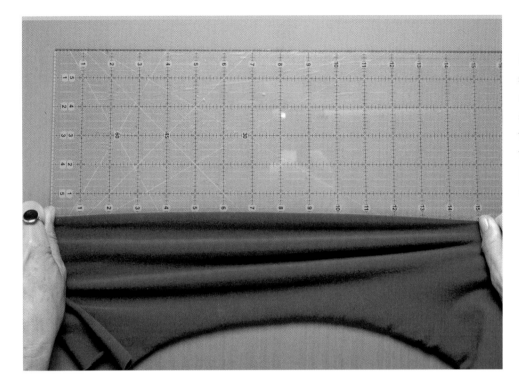

It's easy to test each stretch fabric to determine its percentage of stretch. If 10 in. of fabric stretches easily to 17½ in., the fabric has 75 percent stretch.

you've had some experience working with stretch fabrics.

Using a ruler or tape measure, it's easy to determine how much stretch a fabric has in each direction. Test the stretch both horizontally and vertically, since most fabrics have more stretch one way than the other. In fact, some have stretch in one direction and none in the other. As a general rule, you'll place the direction of greater stretch going around the body, so the stretch of your particular fabric may also affect the pattern layout.

To determine how much a fabric stretches, start by folding the fabric crosswise, about 12 in. from the cut end. Lay 10 in. of the folded edge along the first 10 in. of the ruler. Holding the left side of the fabric stationary, stretch the fabric with your right hand as far as it will comfortably go (see the photo above). If the fabric stretches easily to

12½ in., it has 25 percent stretch; if it stretches to 15 in., it has 50 percent stretch; if it stretches to 17½ in., it has 75 percent stretch; and so on. To test a fabric's lengthwise stretch, fold the fabric parallel to the selvages and repeat the procedure.

If you're using a pattern designed for tricot or stable cotton knit (with 25 percent stretch) and want to substitute a Lycra-blend fabric (with 50 percent to 100 percent stretch), be aware that you'll need to adjust the pattern to be smaller. A stretchy fabric requires little or no ease, or even a negative amount of ease (smaller than the body), and will still move with the body and be quite comfortable to wear. Make a new paper pattern to reflect the changes, and label it "for fabrics with XX percent stretch."

For your first try at making a garment in a Lycra blend from a pattern designed for knits with less stretch, use

The Skinny on Shoulder Pads

You might not associate shoulder pads with lingerie, but think again. In my opinion, they almost qualify as innerwear. Many women wear at least a small shoulder pad in their clothing, not only to balance the proportions but also to help support the weight and shape of a garment. But shoulder pads can present a number of challenges: Which shape and size to wear with each garment? Where to get them? How to attach them? I can suggest two simple solutions: Make use of shoulder pads built into a camisole or attach them to your bra straps.

When you combine a camisole with shoulder pads, like the one shown above made of cotton lace, they'll be smoothly and securely in place for every garment you wear over it, and it's an easy garment to construct. Stretch & Sew 2072 includes a unique camisole pattern with raglan-sleeve lines and a slightly extended shoulder area with a built-in pad. The pattern instructions result in a pad created from several layers of fleece, but you can adjust the number of layers for the thickness you want, which is especially useful when styles dictate a more natural shoulder line.

Another option is to attach removable shoulder pads to your bra straps, using either purchased pads or ones that you sew yourself. This allows you to wear the size and style of pad that suits your shape and garment without sewing a pad into each outfit or being stuck with the pad that comes sewn or Velcroed into every purchased garment.

To make a removable pad that attaches to your bra strap, sew a small strap on the underside of the pad and fasten it either with a snap or with hook-and-loop tape. For the strap, use a 1½-in.- to 2-in.-long strip of ⅜-in.- or ½-in.-wide ribbon, bias tape, or twill tape and a sew-on snap or small piece of hook-and-loop tape. Pin the pad to your bra strap to determine the correct placement with a garment, then turn under the raw ends of the strip and sew one end to the underside of the pad. Sew the hook side of the hook-and-loop tape to the other end of the strip, and sew the loop side to the pad so it lines up with the piece on the strip. Or sew both halves of a snap to the strip and pad.

a couple of sizes smaller than your measurements suggest, then cut out and baste the garment sections together, try it on, and make adjustments as needed. You may not get it exactly right the first time—even clothing designers make a new style more than once—so don't be concerned if you need a second attempt to adjust and make changes. With each experiment, you'll get closer to the perfect fit.

Creating a Pattern

Because I've never studied pattern drafting, my approach to making my own patterns is extremely basic. I frequently use a garment I already own as a guide, which has always been my most direct route to success. To me, a garment that I can try on and measure is much more tangible than working with a paper pattern alone. So if you have a pajama, gown, or other piece of lingerie that you love, consider creating a pattern from it so you can sew it again (and again!).

I've already talked about how relatively simple garment shapes are for most lingerie and loungewear, especially when compared with jackets and other complicated garments with many pattern pieces. For example, most ready-to-wear sleepwear is constructed as quickly and inexpensively as possible, with simple, boxy shapes, few or no darts, and elastic at openings for comfort and shape. (This is why they're easy garments to copy!) It's the fabric, topstitching, and details that make these garments special.

A straight half-slip is a simple garment to copy. Basically a tube with a sewn elastic waist, the slip's fabric, color, and rich lace hem are the details that make this piece special.

Copying from favorite garments is the way I developed patterns for several of the pieces in this book—the pear-print pj shirt shown on p. 32 was copied from a favorite old flannel pj shirt, and the simple brown-print camisole shown on p. 60 was copied from a J. Crew one that I recently bought and loved.

If you'd like to copy one of your favorite lingerie garments, first think about small or large improvements you can make, any changes that will make it even more wonderful to wear. Perhaps it

If you're not ready to cut apart the garment just yet, you can still copy it. One option is to trace the shapes of the garment sections on paper to create pattern pieces. Another way is to find a pattern that's as similar to it as possible, then measure each section of your garment and jot the numbers on a quick rough sketch of each section's shape. Using your measurements and observations, alter the pattern so it's as close as possible to your favorite, including piping, topstitching, pocket and button placement, and other important details.

If the shape is very simple, like my camisoles shown on p. 25 and p. 92, you may not even need to find a similar pattern. Instead, lay the garment flat on pattern paper, side seams together, and draw the front and back pattern shapes on the paper. Then add seam and hem allowances where needed. Cut out the pattern pieces, and you're ready to make the new garment.

If the garment you want to copy is a bra, be persistent; a bra is a more complex garment. Search for the right fabrics and findings, and use the old bra to make a new pattern (see pp. 91–92). And, again, be willing to make the bra more than once if necessary. The results will be worth it.

needs to be an inch or two longer? Or have a smoother finish inside? Or more topstitching to prevent the edges from flopping out? You can fix all these problems now, while you're sewing it again.

Making a copy

If your old garment is worn out, simply cut it apart along the seamlines, clip or remove any elastic, and use the sections to make a new pattern (see the photo above). Smooth out, press, and then trace each section on paper, adding length for hems, drawing on seam allowances where you cut them away, and making any needed improvements.

Make your own easy, custom-drafted patterns for a wrapped half-slip and V-neck camisole, like the ones shown here, which are both cut on the bias and sewn from silk seersucker.

Drafting a new pattern

Another way to create a pattern is called drafting—using your own body measurements to develop a custom pattern. To illustrate how simple this process can be, I'll show you how to create your own patterns for a wrap-style half-slip, a V-neck camisole, and a basic, brief-style panty. The basic panty pattern is the most exciting, I think, because once you create the pattern, it's easy to adjust it to your favorite style, whether you prefer a high-cut leg, a low-cut waist, or a bikini.

Each of the three patterns is designed for knits or woven fabrics (be sure to cut wovens on the bias so they'll be fluid and comfortable). These patternmaking instructions are adapted from the work of Jan Bones, teacher of patternmaking, garment construction, tailoring, and draping at the University of Manitoba in Canada.

Tools for making patterns

To make your own patterns, you'll need some fairly large, paper, a tape measure,

Karen's Closet

While visiting my sister in Galveston, Tex., we used to shop at a fabulous military-surplus store called Colonel Bubbie's. This store stocked absolutely everything (including a genuine NASA space capsule, displayed out front) and was a wonderful place to prowl around. One day I found an incredibly soft, thick, cotton-flannel sleepshirt in a soothing medium blue, with a sort of Nehru collar and utilitarian ring snaps up the asymmetrical front. This English-army pajama shirt turned out to be the most perfect, goofy pj shirt I ever owned. When it started to show wear, I bought another one by mail. These two wonderful shirts lasted for years and became the backbone of my early at-home comfort-clothing outfits.

When the second shirt started to wear out, I panicked. I stitched machine-embroidery on the front in an effort to strengthen it and did other last-ditch mending jobs to keep the shirt going. Finally, when it was too fragile to wear, I washed it one last time and folded it into a ziplock bag, then labeled and stored it in my attic with the intention of making a pattern from it someday and sewing a new, perfect pj shirt. For some reason, I never did, although each time I moved to a new house, that silly shirt went with me. The original English-army shirt is pictured here, and the result (finally!) of my efforts to copy it, the pear-print pajama shirt, is pictured on p. 32. The new shirt is made from fabric that, if possible, is even softer and thicker than the original. My only style change was to lengthen and curve the hemline to create shirttails; the original had a straight hem.

a ruler (I prefer a large, clear plastic ruler like the 6-in. by 24-in. one from Omni-grid shown on p. 70, so I can see what I'm doing), and a pencil. Also have handy your basic body measurements described earlier in this chapter. You can purchase a roll of gridded pattern paper (see Resources on p. 135), which is perfect for the task, or a reasonably priced roll of medical examining-table paper at medical-supply stores. There's also a patternmaking material called Mönster paper, made from a strong synthetic similar to Tyvek. The advantage of Mönster paper is that it's nearly indestructible; you can fit the pattern by actually basting it together and trying it on before cutting out your fabric.

All these options are great, but I sometimes end up simply using freezer paper. It's sturdy, inexpensive, readily available at grocery stores, and fairly wide (25 in.). If you need wider paper for certain sections, you can easily tape two pieces of paper together. For smaller patterns, don't forget that classic—the sturdy brown paper grocery bag, which makes a very durable pattern.

Tools for Quick, Easy Cutting

Cutting out the pattern and fabric has always been my least favorite part of sewing. It's so slow and so permanent—what if I make a mistake? Or what if I change my mind? For this reason, I was happy to discover a quicker and easier way to cut using a rotary cutter and cutting mat. This method is not only faster (no pinning) but also more accurate, since scissors lift the fabric from the table when you cut, which can stretch and distort the fabric and shift the cutting line. And accuracy can be very important in a garment with lots of small pieces, like a bra.

If you still enjoy the scissors-and-pins method, that's okay. But if you're curious about using a rotary cutter, I encourage you to try it. You won't be sorry! A large cutting mat to fit your table surface is an investment; these are available in various sizes and styles from suppliers such as Sew/Fit Company (see Resources on p. 135) and will last for years. Instead of using pins to hold the pattern in place, get some weights designed for this purpose or use small, heavy items found around your house, like short food cans, fabric-paint bottles, or CD cases.

For anchoring small, curvy pieces like bras, use small, round weights or flexible ones such as Wiggle Weights (the black tubes shown at right), available from Élan Patterns. You'll still need your scissors for cutting small curves, notches, and clips—it's easy to cut too far with the rotary cutter. Be sure to change your cutter blade whenever it becomes dull.

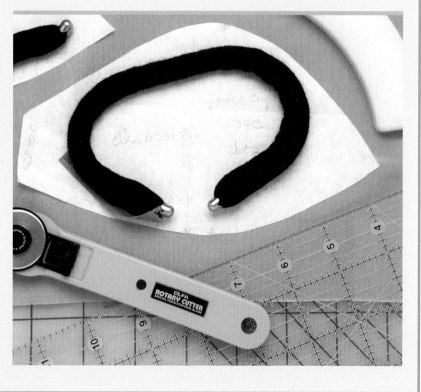

A Wrapped Half-Slip Pattern

The many benefits of slips make them a staple of the well-stocked lingerie drawer. Not only do slips provide some opacity for sheer garments, but they also help the garment hang more smoothly through the waist and hips, reduce wrinkling, and even add warmth and absorb perspiration. Luckily, then, a half-slip is the simplest lingerie pattern

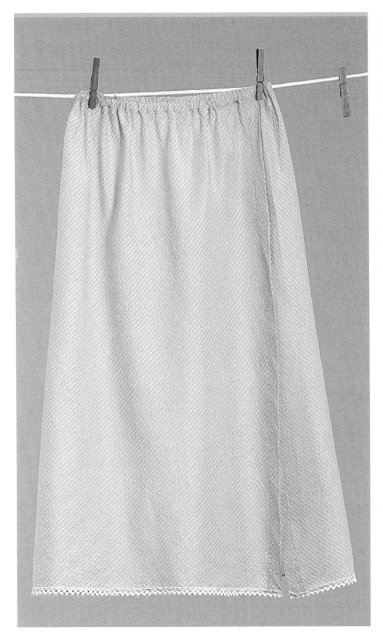

A wrapped half-slip is the easiest pattern to sew. Although the slip is quick to make, a beautiful fabric and fine detail like a sewn casing at the waist and lace at the hem make it a pleasure to wear.

to create, as well as the easiest piece of lingerie to sew because it consists of just one or two rectangles of fabric. The slip described here has a wrapped, over-lap design that creates a comfortable vent, which you can wear at the front, side, or back.

The only measurements you'll need are your hip measurement and your desired finished length. The directions vary depending on the width of your fabric; following are two sets of instructions for both wider and more average widths. For woven fabrics, you'll cut the slip in two pieces on the bias.

Drafting a half-slip pattern for wider fabrics

For knit fabrics from 54 in. to 60 in. wide, you can generally cut the slip in a single large rectangle, depending on your hip measurement. If your full hip measures 36 in. or less, you can fit this pattern on a 45-in.-wide knit fabric; if your full hip measures 46 in. or more, you'll need a 60-in.-wide fabric to use this one-piece pattern.

1 Add 9 in. (23cm) to your hip circum-ference. This is the width of the rectangle.

2 Measure the length for your slip, adding 1 in. or so at the waist for an elastic casing if desired and extra length for a hem if needed. (The yel-low seersucker slip shown on p. 14 has a turned lace hem, so no extra length was needed.) This is the length of the rectangle.

Creating a Half-Slip Pattern

This easy half-slip wraps to create a vent at the hem, which can be worn at the center front, side, or back. Use the measurement for your hip at the widest part. Measure the desired length for the slip. For a knit, place the direction of greater stretch going around the body.

For wider fabrics:
Cut one rectangle according to the illustration.

For narrower fabrics and wovens:
Cut two rectangles as shown, placing the rectangle on the bias for a woven fabric.

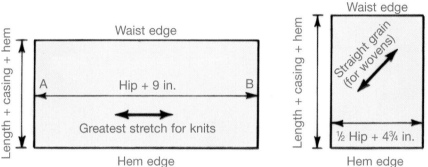

3 Draw a rectangle on pattern paper as shown in the left illustration above, taping two pieces of paper together if needed.

And that's your pattern! For instructions on assembling the slip, see the sidebar on p. 76.

Drafting a half-slip pattern for narrow or woven fabrics

In addition to narrower knits (less than your hip plus 9 in.), use this two-piece pattern for wovens such as silk and cotton batiste. Since most woven fabrics aren't wide enough to allow cutting the large rectangle on the bias, you'll need to cut the slip in two pieces. It's easy to join them before proceeding with the construction.

1 Divide your hip measurement in half and add 4¾ in. (12cm) or more (soft or slippery fabrics may stretch to become longer/narrower on the bias). This is the width of the rectangle.

2 Measure the desired length for the slip, and add 1 in. for an elastic casing if desired and extra length for a hem if needed. This is the length of the rectangle.

Constructing a Wrapped Half-Slip

When cutting your slip from a knit fabric, place the pattern's horizontal arrow in the direction of greater stretch. When cutting your slip from a woven fabric, place the diagonal arrow along the straight grain of the fabric.

1 If you've cut your slip in two pieces, first sew the side seam to join the two pieces, using one of the seam options discussed in chapter 3.

2 Turn under 1 in. (2.5cm) at A and B (see the illustration at right), and topstitch. A multiple zigzag stitch makes an attractive finish.

3 Finish the hem edge with lace, ribbon, or a narrow hem, choosing one of the hem options discussed in chapter 3.

4 At the waist, measure in 3⅛ in. (8cm) from the A edge and mark, then measure down 7½ in. (19cm) from the top edge and mark. Lap B over A to the marks, creating an overlap, and pin.

5 Choose one of several options to anchor the overlap:

❑ Stitch over the first line of stitching used to hem B to the second mark.

❑ Sew one or two embroidery motifs in the overlap area.

❑ Appliqué a piece of ribbon or lace of any size; this can be cut from a larger piece of lace. Stitch it in place using a narrow zigzag to outline the motif.

6 Finish the waist with elastic, using one of the options discussed in chapter 3. An elastic casing with ½-in.-wide elastic makes a nice, smooth waistline for a half-slip.

Constructing a Slip

After hemming the edges at A and B, finish the hem, wrap side B over side A, and anchor the overlap with appliqué or stitching. Finish the waist with elastic as desired.

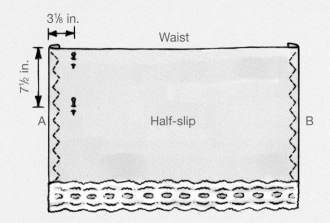

3 Draw a rectangle on paper as shown in the right illustration on p. 75. For a knit fabric, draw a horizontal line to indicate the direction of greater stretch. For a woven fabric, fold the pattern lengthwise and crosswise, then match these foldlines to locate the bias grainline. Draw it on the pattern. Draw a seccond rectangle the same as the first.

This is your pattern. See the instructions for assembling the slip in the sidebar on the facing page.

A V-Neck Camisole Pattern

It's also easy to make a camisole pattern that's custom-fitted to your body. This versatile camisole style has a V-neck, side seams, and narrow straps (see the photo at right). To make the pattern, you'll need just four body measurements: the bust, high hip, bust to waist, and bust level to high hip (or desired length).

The illustration on p. 78 may look complicated, but the process is simple. You'll be drawing the camisole front and back on one sheet. When finished, trace the camisole back so you'll have a separate pattern piece for it.

A soft cotton knit is a perfect fabric to use for a custom camisole pattern. The upper edge has piping with a simple facing, and elastic gives a closer fit at the upper back.

On a large sheet of paper, draw the following lines in order:

1 0 to 1: Bust level to high hip (or length desired).

2 0 to 2: Bust level to waist; mark.

3 1 to 3: High hip plus 1⅝ in. (4cm), divided by 4.

4 0 to 4: Bust plus 1⅝ in. (4cm), divided by 4.

A Custom Camisole Pattern

The camisole has a V-neck and narrow straps.
To make pattern, you need four body measurements:
bust, high hip, bust to waist, and bust level to high hip
(or desired length). Line lengths correspond to these key
measurements, as directed.

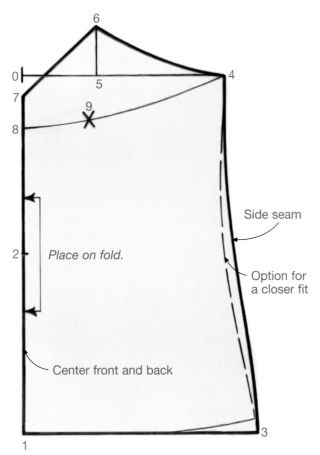

Side seam

Option for
a closer fit

Place on fold.

Center front and back

5 4 to 3: Join in a smooth curve (you can add more shape at the waist if desired).

6 At 3, raise the hem ¼ in. to ⅜ in. (0.5cm to 0.8cm) to create a smooth corner.

7 0 to 5: Measure on the body from the center front to the preferred strap location (usually directly above the bust point).

8 5 to 6: 4 in. to 4¾ in. (10cm to 12cm), measured straight up to the desired peak of front.

9 0 to 7: ¾ in. to 1¼ in. (2cm to 3cm) for front V. Join 7 to 6 with a straight line, then join 6 to 4 with a gentle curve.

10 0 to 8: 2¾ in. to 3⅝ in. (7cm to 9cm). Join 8 to 4 in a soft curve to shape the upper back.

11 Locate the back strap about 2¾ in. to 3⅝ in. (7cm to 9cm) from the center back.

Be sure to add seam allowances to the pattern where needed. For a knit fabric, you may want ¼-in. seam allowances at the sides and upper edges; for a woven, I suggest 1-in. or wider side seams so you'll have room for adjusting if needed. Choose a hem from the options given in chapter 3, and add a hem allowance if needed. I sometimes use a turned lace hem, which doesn't require additional length.

Another set of "ideal" innerwear: This easy camisole and French-cut panty, sewn from a lustrous Austrian cotton knit, would command high prices in stores.

A Basic Panty Pattern

The perfect pair of panties can be one of the most difficult garments to buy, no matter how much you're willing to spend. There are dozens of different cuts and styles in stores, and finding the same one you love the next time you shop can be nearly impossible. Using the following instructions and your body measurements, you can develop the perfect panty pattern for your body, eliminating this frustrating search. And it's not difficult!

When you shop for panties, you'll see that most are made from a knit fabric for comfort, either cotton knit, a Lycra-blend knit, or nylon tricot. The more stretch the fabric has, the smaller the pattern can be. For the first pair you make, I suggest starting with a stable knit that has 25 percent stretch. Later you can experiment and adjust for more stretchy knits, as explained on p. 66. Regardless of the fabric you choose for the panty, always cut the inner crotch section from a soft, thin cotton knit for comfort and absorbency.

You'll begin with four body measurements: the waist, hip, waist-to-hip length, and crotch depth. On a large piece of paper, draw the following lines as shown in the illustration at right.

Creating a Basic, Custom Panty Pattern

Drafting your own panty pattern gives you the freedom to get just what you want. Begin with body measurements for waist, hip, waist to hip, and crotch depth. Line lengths correspond to these key measurements, as directed.

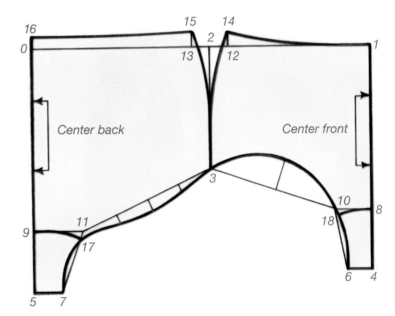

CONSTRUCTING A V-NECK CAMISOLE

For a simple camisole in a knit fabric, cut the front and back pattern pieces on the fold, with the direction of greater stretch going around the body. For woven fabrics, you'll need to cut the fabric in a single layer. Make a full pattern by flipping the pattern at the center foldline and drawing the second half on paper; do the same for the back pattern. Fold each pattern piece as described for the bias-cut half-slip on p. 77, then draw a diagonal grainline, and place it on the straight grain of the fabric.

If you're planning to cut the camisole on the bias, another option is to add center-front and center-back seams, which allows you to create a chevron effect with a striped fabric, as I did (see the photo below). Don't forget to add seam allowances at the centers. Again, cut the fabric in a single layer, placing each side-front and side-back in alternating directions on the stripes, reversing the pattern piece. Another interesting option for knits or wovens is to cut the pattern longer and wider at the hem to create a chemise full-slip or nightgown.

To sew the camisole, use one of the seam options discussed in chapter 3. I experimented with narrow French seams for the yellow seersucker camisole, but found them to be too stiff in this fabric. Instead, I settled on a plain, straight-stitched seam, pressed open. Because the bias doesn't ravel, you don't need an additional edge finish. To build some give into the seam, stretch it slightly while stitching.

To finish the front V-neckline, you have several options. For a knit or woven, you can lap and sew on narrow lace, folding to create mitered corners at the inner and outer points. Hand-sew the folds in place, and trim the excess.

Another option is to cut a 2-in.-wide bias facing for the front, using the upper edge of the camisole front as a pattern. Finish the facing's inner edge by serging, binding, turning under and stitching, or straight stitching, then pinking the edge, depending on how much the fabric ravels. Or you can create an invisible finish by facing the facing with a thin fabric such as silk organza. To do this, cut a facing from each fabric. With right sides together,

Adding center-front and center-back seams to the camisole pattern and cutting the sections on the bias allow you to create chevrons using a striped fabric. Be sure to lay adjacent sections in opposite directions on the fabric to form the chevron.

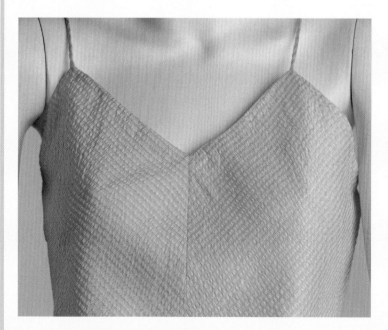

sew the inner edge, then press, clip the curves, and turn. Baste the raw edges together, and it's ready to join to the garment.

Constructing the camisole

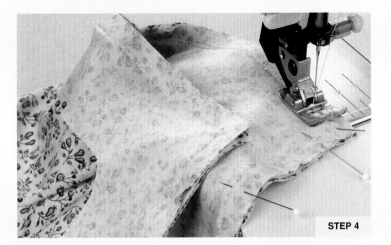

STEP 4

1 Join the center-back and center-front seams if you have them.

2 Finish the upper-back edge with narrow elastic that is cut to be 90 percent as long as the fabric edge. Sew to the upper-back edge, using a

turned application (see p. 49). Clear tape elastic makes a nice, thin edge.

3 Next, choose a strap from the options in chapter 3. A spaghetti strap (as narrow as ⅛ in.) works well. Pin a strap to each peak, matching raw edges.

4 With right sides together, sew the facing to the front, catching the strap in the seam. Open out the facing, press the seam allowances toward the facing, then understitch close to the seam as far as possible

5 Press the facing in place, then top-stitch the front from the right side, 1 in. from the edge, sewing from the peak of one side to the other.

6 Turn in and hand-sew the ends of the facing to the side seams.

7 Choose a hem option from the ideas given in chapter 3.

When sewing the facing to the upper edge of the camisole, insert the straps into the seam so they'll be caught in the stitching. Backstitch across the straps again to secure them.

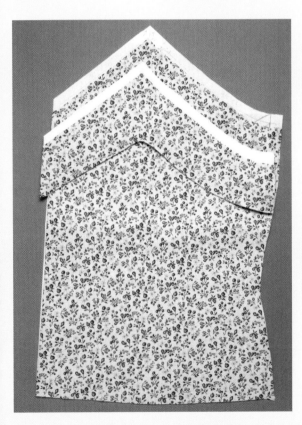

It's easy to make a simple facing pattern using the upper edge of the camisole as a guide. Measure 2 in. away and draw a smooth line to complete the facing pattern.

For the body:

1 0 to 1: Hip measurement divided by 2, minus 1 to 1½ in. (2.5cm to 3.5cm), depending on the fabric stretch.

2 0 to 2: (one-half of the measurement from 0 to 1) plus ¾ in. (2cm).

3 2 to 3: Waist to hip minus ¾ in. (2cm).

4 1 to 4: Crotch depth plus 3¼ in. (8cm).

5 0 to 5: Crotch depth plus 4¾ in. (12cm).

6 4 to 6 and 5 to 7: 1⅜ in. to 1⅝ in. (3.5cm to 4cm).

7 4 to 8: 4¾ in. (12cm).

8 5 to 9: 4 in. (10cm).

9 8 to 10: 2 in. to 2¼ in. (5cm to 5.5cm).

10 9 to 11: 3¾ in. to 4 in. (9.5cm to 10cm).

To shape the leg, draw guidelines from 6 to 10 to 3 to 11 to 7, as follows:

1 6 to 10: Inward ¼ in. (0.5cm).

2 10 to 3: Inward 2 in. to 2½ in. (5cm to 6cm).

3 3 to 11: Mark in quarters, and curve out ¾ in. to 1 in. at the center as shown.

4 11 to 7: Curve inward ¼ in. to ½ in. (0.5 to 1cm).

Shape the waist:

5 Hip minus waist = x.

6 x minus ease of 3¼ in. to 4¾ in. (8cm to 12cm) = y.

7 y divided by 4 = z.

8 z = amount of shaping used at the front and back side seams.

9 2 to 12 and 2 to 13 = z.

10 12 to 14, 13 to 15, and 0 to 16 = ½ in. to ¾ in. (1.5cm to 2cm).

11 Join 15 to 16 and 14 to 1.

For example, for a 37-in. (92cm) hip and 27-in. (68cm) waist: 37 minus 27 in. = 10 in. (x). 10 in. minus 4 in. of ease = 6 in. (y). 6 divided by 4 = 1½ in. (z).

Shape the side seam by joining 14 and 15 to vertical line 2 to 3 in a gentle curve.

tip. . .

For a customized fit when sewing the elastic to the panty leg, allow less fullness at the front of the leg and more fullness at the back. This helps to prevent the panty from riding up in back.

Constructing a Basic Panty

Once you've completed the basic panty pattern, it's easy to customize the waist and leg shaping to get just the style you want. To create your perfect panty, the first step is to cut and sew a basic-style panty from the pattern you've drafted. (Use scrap fabric if you don't plan to wear it.) The following instructions, together with the pattern you've drawn, will result in a basic, to-the-waist panty that fits your body.

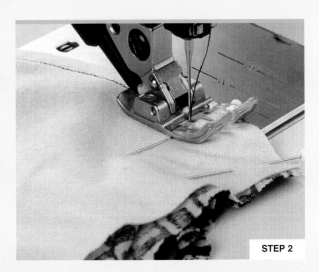

STEP 2

1 Cut the panty front, back, and crotch piece from fashion fabric, and cut a second crotch piece from thin cotton knit.

2 For the front crotch seam, place the right side of the outer crotch section to the right side of the panty front, and place the right side of the inner cotton crotch section to the wrong side of the panty front. Pin the three layers together and stitch. Fold the crotch pieces away from the panty and press.

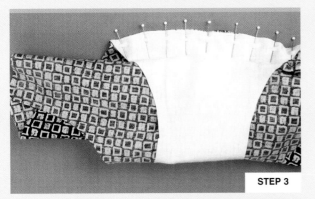

STEP 3

3 Place the back crotch pieces on either side of the back panty seam in the same way, wrapping the second crotch piece around the rolled panty sections. Sew through all layers, turn it right side out, and press.

4 With right sides together, sew the panty side seams using one of the seam options discussed in chapter 3.

5 Finish the waist and leg openings with elastic using the turned, bound, or casing method given in chapter 3. Cut the elastic 2 in. to 4 in. (6cm to 10 cm) smaller than your measurement, trying it around your body to decide what is comfortable. To finish a turned-elastic application at the panty waist, use a narrow twin needle and topstitch from the right side, stretching slightly and catching the raw edge in the stitching.

STEP 5

Customizing for Your Own Perfect Shaping

To customize waist and leg shaping, first make a basic brief-style panty, then try it on and draw desired lines for waist and leg height right on the panty.

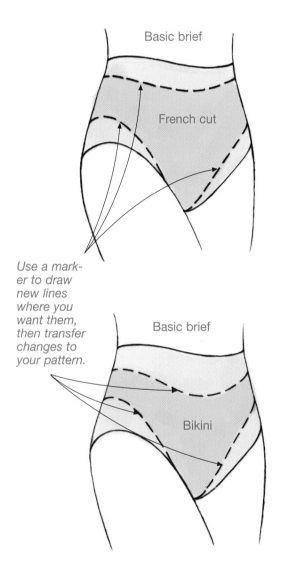

Use a marker to draw new lines where you want them, then transfer changes to your pattern.

Shape the crotch:

1 Back: Measure ½ in. (1cm) below 11 and mark 17. Curve a line from 9 to 17 and cut.

2 Front: Measure ¼ in. (0.5cm) below 10 and mark 18. Curve a line from 8 to 18 and cut. Line up 5 to 7 and 4 to 6 and tape together to form the crotch pattern piece.

3 Optional step for the front panty crotch seam: Tape an extra piece of paper to the panty front at the 8 to 18 line. Measure down ¼ in. to ⅜ in. (0.5cm to 0.8cm) below 18 and curve a line up to 8. This gives a smoother, nonbinding fit in the front leg area.

Complete the pattern:

1 Cut out the drafted pattern pieces for the panty front and back.

2 Trace the pieces and mark the center front and center back as foldlines.

3 Add ¼-in. (0.5cm) seam allowances to the side seams and crotch seams of the front, back, and crotch pieces.

4 If you're using the turned method of applying elastic, add seam allowances the width of the elastic at the waist and leg edges, including the crotch piece. If you're using the lapped method of applying elastic, add no seam allowances.

Karen's Closet

If you're making panties for yourself, why not have the best? As I discovered, it's not difficult to make a long-lasting, high-quality panty that looks a lot like a fine European import.

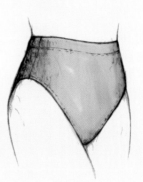

For my own ideal panty, a modified French-cut style, I raised the leg about 3 in. at the side front, tapering it to the crotch area. I left the top edge at the waist and used wide elastic for a slight tummy-controlling effect, as I've seen in ready-to-wear. A silky, tightly knitted Austrian cotton knit plus turned, covered elastic with tiny twin-needle top-stitching gave my panties the polish of the $20 Swiss-made ones, exactly the effect that I wanted.

Adapting the pattern for your preferences

After you've constructed a basic panty, you're ready to adapt the pattern for your perfect panty shape. Whether you want a high-cut leg, a lowered waist, or a bikini, try on the panty you've sewn and use a washable, felt-tip marker to draw lines where you'd like the panty lines to fall on your body. Take it off and transfer these lines to your pattern, measuring from the original edges to your new marked lines.

Next, trace the pattern to create a new one (while preserving the basic pattern you've already created for future reference), and add the needed seam allowance at each edge. Chapter 3 explains a number of options for adding elastic and finishing edges and the seam allowance widths required for each. As you sew each new pair of panties, take careful notes of what works (and what doesn't) to use again on your next pair.

Now that you know how to create your own patterns, can it be any harder to make a bra? In the next chapter, I'll explore the fitting and construction steps you'll need to sew your own perfect bra.

ALL ABOUT BRAS

One of the most satisfying lingerie garments to sew is the everyday bra. Not only do many women have a hard time finding a bra that fits, but it also can be difficult to find the same style again next time you shop, since manufacturers frequently discontinue styles in their lines. Sewing one yourself has several advantages: Aside from getting the perfect fit, it can be in the fabric and color of your choice as well.

Getting that perfect fit, however, requires accuracy. Because a bra is so fitted, a mere ⅛-in. cutting or sewing error can throw it off a whole cup size. But don't worry—a bra is not difficult to sew. If you can cut accurately and sew a precise ¼-in. seam, you can make a successful bra. And after you've perfected the fit, sewing a bra from start to finish can take just two hours or less. That's about how long it takes to drive to a mall, find a parking place, and try on a pile of ready-to-wear bras!

In this chapter, with the help of bra expert Cindy Elam of Élan Patterns, a company that specializes in bra patterns, you'll learn what you need to make the perfect bra for your body every time. But before diving into specific information about fitting, I'll take a look at bra styling options, patterns, fabrics, and findings that make a great bra.

Anatomy of a Bra

Variations in the four basic elements of a bra—bra band, cup, strap, and closure determine bra style.

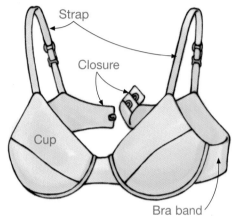

Strap

Closure

Cup

Bra band

Anatomy of a Bra—Which Style Is Right for You?

Every woman is familiar with the four basic parts of a bra: cup, band, straps, and closure (see the illustration above). What you may not realize is that variations in these four basic elements determine the bra style. Depending on your body type, your activity level, the occasion, and your personal preferences, you can choose the style that suits you best.

Bra bands

The bra band provides the foundation for the bra and supports most of the bust's weight. It can be a full-band style, which encircles the body and has the

Comfort Zone

If bra straps tend to cut into your shoulders, as they do for many women with large or heavy breasts, there are several things you can do to correct this problem. When sewing your own bras, you can make wider, more comfortable straps that support the weight more evenly without cutting into your shoulders. Élan pattern B530 offers a smooth, wide self-fabric strap, and it's easy to add a layer of batting to the strap, if you'd like it to be padded, before turning it.

Another option is to sew a separate bra-strap pad that you can attach onto any bra you're wearing. The one I've seen for sale in catalogs is about 2½ in. by 7 in., and the ends come to a soft point so they don't show under garments. It's made from two layers of fleece or batting sandwiched between two layers of fabric, then finished around the edges using a serger or a zigzag or overlock stitch. The pad attaches beneath the strap with a flap that's sewn to the pad on one edge and has a hook-and-loop closure on the other. It's an easy-to-make and very functional bra accessory.

cups set into it, or a partial band, which is attached at the cup's sides, with a small center-front section that joins the cups. A full-band style offers more support and is a good choice for everyday wear for the fuller figure. Regardless of the style, the band should be comfortably snug around the body.

Cups

Bra cups cover and support the breasts and mold their shape. A cup can be made of a single seamless piece or constructed from two, three, or more lined or unlined pieces. The most common cup style has two sections. Cups may or may not include underwires for shaping, which increase the bra's support.

In a good-fitting bra, the breasts should fill the cups completely with no wrinkling or excess fabric and no breast tissue spilling over the top or at the sides or bottom of the cup. The center section should lie close to the breastbone, giving good separation of the breasts. A bra that stretches in a nearly straight line from bust point to bust point like a hammock does not provide proper support.

A full cup bra is the basic, everyday style for many women. Variations such as the demi or French cup are cut lower, offer less support, and are better suited to a smaller-busted figure. If you'd like to create the look of a fuller bust, you can choose a padded or push-up style pattern. Or you can add a layer of batting (my favorite is Pellon fusible fleece) to any cup style.

Straps

The bra strap provides lift to the bra cup and the breast. Straps may be made of the same fabric as the bra, of a nonstretch strapping material, or of strap elastic, the most common choice. A nonstretch strap typically includes an elastic insert at the back, so the strap will have some give.

The straps should rest comfortably on your shoulders without digging in or slipping off. Straps that dig into your shoulder indicate that too much weight is hanging from them due to cups that are too small, a band that's too loose or too narrow, or a combination of these. If, after correcting the fit of the band and cups, the straps still leave dents in your shoulders, try changing to a wider, padded strap that distributes the weight over a larger area, like the left bra shown on p. 86. Or make a bra-strap pad (see the sidebar on the facing page).

Straps that slip off your shoulders are either set too far apart for your body type or need to be shortened. If shortening doesn't correct the problem, you can easily alter your pattern to a style with straps set closer together in back (see "Converting a Bra Pattern to a Racer or V-Back" on pp. 103–107).

Closures

Every basic bra has either a back or a front closure. For a front-closing bra, used only on a partial-band style, the center-front piece has a nonadjustable

tip. . .

Starting with a full-coverage bra pattern, you can create a more attractive style that you still won't spill out of when you bend over by making the bra slightly lower in front. Redraw the lines on your pattern pieces to reduce the height of the center-front section, and deepen the angle of the cup's upper edge to match. If you change the pattern a lot, you may need to shorten the length of the underwire.

plastic or nylon clasp or hook assembly. A back closure works equally well with a full- or partial-band-style bra. The hook side of the closure is attached on the right side (as it's worn) and the eyes on the left, with the option of one or more sets of hooks/eyes, depending on how much support is needed. Even though the bra is being custom-fitted to your body, it's still nice to have a choice of two or three hook settings to accommodate weight gain or loss and monthly fluctuations.

Options for Bra Patterns

When you start to look at bra patterns, you'll notice that most of the ones on the market are for basic styles because that's what women sew and wear the most. You'll find basic partial-band styles, full-coverage bras, sports bras, and demi or push-up styles. You can also adapt a pattern to achieve several of the variations mentioned, including a minimizer, racer or V-back, more attractive full-coverage bra, padded bra, and sports bra with firmer support, by using the tips and instructions in this chapter.

What's Your Style?

The type of bra style that suits you best is determined by several factors. Aside from the obvious body type, there's also personal taste and the occasion to consider. In other words, where are you going and what will you be wearing?

❏ **Sports bras.** For vigorous exercise like jogging or aerobics, you'll want a sports bra that provides good support. Most sports bras rely on compression to reduce bouncing and are designed with the cups, straps, and a wider-than-usual band cut all in one piece with no closure. If you're looking for firm support in a sports bra, I suggest that you use a Lycra-blend fabric, add a full lining or underlining, and make the fit snug like the one shown at top on p. 8.

❏ **Strapless bras.** For a strapless or spaghetti-strap dress, choose a strapless bra, perhaps a long-line style for more formal occasions. In ready-to-wear, I see a number of strapless bras that are little more than snug tube tops of bra width with elastic at the top and bottom. This easy style is perfect for a smaller-busted figure wearing a casual summer dress.

❏ **Demi-style/push-up bras.** Women with average-to-small, firm breasts can wear nearly any style. Many young, fashion-conscious women prefer the demi-style and "miraculous" push-up bras with straps that attach near the front armhole edge of the bra for the slinglike support that helps create cleavage. If you'd like to sew this style, you may want to convert the pattern to a racer or V-back (see the instructions on pp. 103–107) to prevent the straps from falling off your shoulders.

Creating a Minimizer Bra

Adjust the pattern to create the effect of a minimizer bra by reshaping the cups to flatten the bust point and redistribute some of the fullness to the sides.

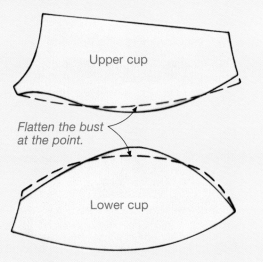

Upper cup

Flatten the bust at the point.

Lower cup

❏ **Full-coverage bras.** As women age, factors such as gravity, nursing babies, and menopause can cause breast tissue to become softer and lose elasticity. A full-coverage bra can be a better choice for softer breast tissue, while a very full bust is best in a full-coverage bra with a full band, underwires, and good support. But this doesn't have to look like a bra your grandmother wore—it can be made of lace or in a fun color you love. Many attractive styles provide adequate lift, support, and coverage. For more tips, see p. 105.

❏ **Minimizer bras.** If your shirts tend to gap between the bustline buttons, try sewing a minimizer bra. This style has a cup that's less pointed at the bust tip, distributing some of the fullness to the sides. You can duplicate this effect on your pattern by redrawing the cups as shown in the illustration above.

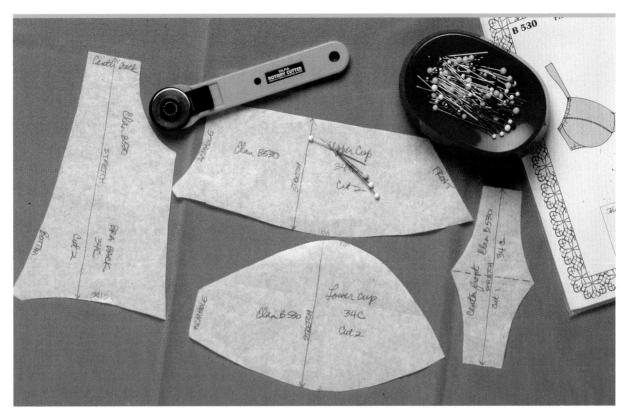

When making your own bra pattern, either traced from a purchased pattern or from a garment you're copying, be sure to label essential details on each piece such as the location of the strap, armhole edge, center front, top, and bottom, so it will be easy to orient the piece in the garment as you sew.

All the patterns I've tried have thorough, well-illustrated instructions. But to avoid unwelcome surprises, always read the entire instructions before you even begin to cut your fabric. You'll find companies that sell bra patterns listed in Resources on p. 135.

Re-creating your favorite bra

Many of us have at least one bra that's close to perfect, and if so, it's often been worn to the point of wearing it out. As with panties discussed in the previous chapter, it makes sense to try to copy it. One method is to adapt an existing pattern to be as close as possible to your favorite. For some helpful, basic information, see "Creating a Pattern" on pp. 69–73.

Yet a bra is not as simple to copy as a sleep shirt. It tends to have small pieces and a close, three-dimensional fit. The fit of the cup is the most crucial part. Start by cutting one side of the old bra apart along the seamlines, snipping through the elastic so the band will lie flat, then lay the pieces on paper and trace around them. Label your drawings carefully to note the location of the strap, armhole edge, center front, and other important details (see the photo above). Study a pattern for a similar bra to learn how much seam allowance to add at each edge and to understand the construction order. You can use the uncut other half of the bra as a helpful reference for details and to see how

Perhaps like many other women, I've never loved wearing a bra. But endless trips to lingerie departments didn't offer much in the way of alternatives. I needed something that was comfortable and smooth under clothing but also snug and firm enough to offer some support.

Finally, I found a plain, black workout/exercise top that fit my needs exactly—it was a simple shape, made from a firm, stretchy cotton/Lycra knit, and ended just at the waist. The wide straps stayed in place, and all the edges were turned under and finished with twin-needle stitching. Perfect! It solved a problem, and I quickly became hooked on its comfort and functionality. But when I went searching for more of these tops to buy, I couldn't find any others that fit correctly—they were all too big! So I made a paper pattern from the original black one, bought some cotton/Lycra knit fabrics, and made myself a batch of "workout" camisoles.

If you'd like to try a snug-fitting camisole as a bra substitute, start with a camisole pattern designed for knits or a pattern for a workout top. Or simply copy the shape from a top that fits you, as I did. Make the fit snug to offer some support or add a shelf bra, as explained below. Firm cotton/Lycra fabrics work well for this type of garment because they stretch and recover well.

seams were finished. Note the layers and types of fabric and findings used.

If you aren't ready to give up your favorite bra, make paper tracings and detailed measurements of the garment sections. Use this information to adapt the pattern for a similar bra to get as close to your favorite as possible.

When you're ready to transfer your ideas to fabric, always make a sample cup and fit it on yourself before you continue (see p. 98). And be willing to make the bra more than once if necessary. Since small amounts of both fabric and time are invested in sewing a bra,

purchase enough materials to make several. Get as close as possible on the first try, and then fine-tune the fit until you have just the bra you want. You will not regret the time you've invested because you'll have a permanent, custom-fitted bra pattern that you can sew again and again.

Adding a shelf bra to a snug camisole

I've talked about the idea of wearing a snug-fitting camisole as a bra substitute. To make a fitted camisole with even more support, try adding a soft shelf bra, like the ones seen in swimwear.

An easy shelf bra is like a supportive lining for the camisole or top that ends under the bustline. Sew a band of plush elastic along the lower edge for support.

This built-in support option is often found in ready-to-wear camisoles and tank tops, and it is an easy feature to add to your own fitted camisoles and tops.

Make the shelf-bra section using the pattern front for your camisole or top, but cut it shorter. Using a thin, supportive knit fabric (cotton/Lycra knit works well), cut it the same as the front through the neck and armhole area, but end the shelf-bra section below the bust, adding a narrow seam allowance.

1 Cut plush lingerie elastic about 90 percent as long as the under-bust front body measurement. Lap and sew the elastic to the lower edge of the shelf-bra section using a zigzag stitch, stretching the elastic slightly to fit.

2 With wrong sides together, baste the raw edges of this shelf-bra section to the camisole front, then continue with the camisole construction as

For your first sewn bra, a stretch fabric like two-way stretch nylon/Lycra satin makes fitting easier and forgives small errors.

usual, finishing the raw edges with lace, a binding, elastic, or a narrow, twin-needle hem.

For even greater support, you can also construct the shelf bra to extend all the way around the body, as on the top shown at right in the bottom photo on p. 8. This variation is made the same way, except that you cut both front and back shelf-bra sections using the front and back pattern pieces, and join them at the side seams. Cut elastic to 90 percent of the under-bust measurement, sew it into a loop, mark both the elastic and shelf bra in quarters, then lap and join. Complete the camisole as in step 2 on p. 93 and above.

Your Choice of Fabrics

Women's bras can be, and have been, made of practically any wearable substance, from leather and vinyl to silk and cotton. Obviously, some are more comfortable for everyday wear than others. Today, the most popular bra fabrics include knits such as nylon/Lycra satin and cotton knits. A knit fabric allows the bra to give, which makes fitting easier and adds comfort and wearing ease. Fabrics containing Lycra provide extra support and recovery to knits. A Lycra fabric such as Power Net provides the

most support and is often used for the bra band. Another comfortable option for bra fabric is a woven that's blended with Lycra, such as the charcoal silk/Lycra bra shown on p. 111.

Stretch, or raschel, lace and stabilized, nonstretch lace also frequently appear in bra construction. Stretch lace is softer and typically doesn't require lining, but if you want to line it for more stability, use a sheer 15-denier nylon tricot, paying attention to the direction of greater stretch (see the sidebar "Adding Support for a Large Bust" on p. 105). Stabilized lace can be a bit scratchier than stretch, so add a soft, sheer stabilized nylon underlining.

As for any other garment, check your pattern for the recommended fabrics. Bras designed for regular wovens and other nonstretch fabrics like stabilized lace are less forgiving of errors in fitting and sewing and don't have the comfortable "give" of a knit. But they can provide good support and can offer the cool comfort of 100 percent cotton.

Substituting another fabric in a pattern

When working with a specific bra pattern, it's fine to substitute one fabric in place of another as long as they have similar stretch and recovery, such as cotton/Lycra or panné velvet for nylon/Lycra. You can also substitute a woven cotton in any bra pattern that calls for stabilized lace. But since a bra pattern designed for knits takes the fabric's stretch into account, substituting a nonstretch fabric may require some adjustment. Experiment by using the next larger cup; if there's a little excess, adjust it to fit (see the sidebar "Common Fitting Challenges" on p. 101). Or you can try adding a bit more fullness at the bust point of the cup, tapering to nothing at the sides.

If you try substituting a swimwear knit with stretch in all directions when the pattern specifies a tricot or raschel knit, which stretches in only one direction, you may lose some of the shape and support designed into the pattern. Compensate for this by adding a stabilizer to the cup (see the sidebar on p. 105).

The Facts about Fitting

An accurate set of measurements will give you the information you need to select a size for a sample bra. But before getting started, it's useful to understand the relationship between cup and bra band size, which are directly related. If the cup fits correctly but the band is too loose or tight, your cup size will change if you move up or down a band size in your pattern.

For example, if a 38C cup fits perfectly but the band is too tight, you have two options. You can add to the bra band pattern piece by slashing and spreading it (which is the easiest solution and doesn't affect the cup size), or since the cup on a 40C is larger than a 38C, you can try the size 40B (most bra patterns contain multiple sizes). Conversely, if the band is too loose, you can try the size 36D, or simply fold the band pattern piece to make it smaller. The chart at right shows which cup capacities are approximately equivalent.

This chart can also be helpful for women who wear a hard-to-find size, like 30DD or 42A. Even if the pattern doesn't list the size you need, it's possible to find an alternate size that will work, with moderate adjustments to the band.

Taking your measurements

To make a bra that fits, the first step is to take accurate measurements. If possible, have a second person with you to do the measuring, preferably someone with a bit of experience. (Since your arms need to hang at your sides, it's nearly impossible to take accurate measurements of your own body.) Wear your best-fitting bra, especially if you have a large bust; without support, the measurements won't be accurate.

1 To calculate your bra-band size, measure around your ribcage, directly under your bust. Be sure the tape is smooth and level around your body, and pull it snug but not too tight. Whatever the measurement, add 4 in. or 5 in. to get an even whole number (since that's how bra bands are

Compare bra sizes across a row to determine other sizes that have approximately the same cup capacity.

30C	32B	34A	36AA				
30D	32C	34B	36A				
30DD	32D	34C	36B	38A			
	32DD	34D	36C	38B	40A		
		34DD	36D	38C	40B	42A	
			36DD	38D	40C	42B	44A
				38DD	40D	42C	44B

Bra Fixtures and Findings

Bras contain a number of mysterious components, more than you'll find in most other types of sewing. These elements make a bra seem trickier to sew than it really is. When you study a bra and realize that these little findings can be purchased at your local fabric store or ordered from a lingerie supplier, it takes some of the mystery out of this everyday sewing project. Also, to make gathering and matching the parts even easier, you can dye all the fabric and findings together after sewing the bra, as explained in chapter 6 (and throw in a matching panty, while you're at it). The items you'll need include closures, straps, and underwires.

Closures

A front bra closure is a small nylon or plastic clasp that is sewn onto the center section of a bra. These are available in limited colors and also in clear; the clear ones blend with many bra fabrics. A back bra closure consists of two sew-on sections, one with rows of hooks, the other with rows of eyes. Some hook-and-eye closures have heat-sealed edges so they need only to be sewn to the bra back without further finishing. Others (often sold by the yard) have cut edges that require finishing after they're attached to the bra. Use a satin stitch at the top and bottom raw edges and where the closure attaches to the bra.

For making a bra, you'll need a few special findings. From the top: back-hook closures, strap elastic, plush elastic, rings and slides for adjustable straps, underwires, and channeling.

(Photo by Scott Phillips, courtesy Threads magazine, © The Taunton Press, Inc.)

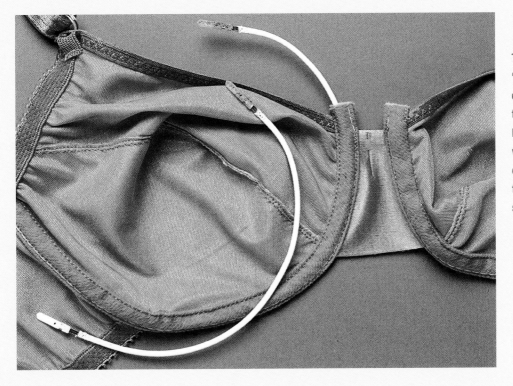

The bra underwire "sits" in a comfy, cushioned band called the channeling. Inserting the underwire and stitching the channeling closed is the final step in constructing a bra.

Straps

You can make straps from a variety of materials, including the bra self-fabric, but the most frequent choice is strap elastic. Strap elastic is less stretchy than other types of elastic, so it provides good support. A bra strap also needs a little metal or plastic ring and a slide. The ring joins the strap to the bra, while the slide makes the strap adjustable.

Underwires

Metal underwires look like a form of medieval torture, but they're actually quite functional. They help support the bust and maintain the shape of the cup, and if the bra fits correctly, they can be downright comfortable. Underwires come in sizes to match your bra size and in full-cup and demi-cup lengths. To "capture" the underwire and keep it

from poking through the bra, you need something called channeling. This folded, padded casing is sold by the yard and sewn around the bra cup to hold the underwire in place.

Another important bra component is plush elastic, which is fuzzy on one side with one picot edge of tiny decorative loops. It's used for finishing the bra's edges.

Since it can be difficult or impossible to find all these ingredients in colors to match your bra fabric, you may want to buy everything in white and dye your own bra and findings in the washing machine, before or after sewing. If you're using a nylon/Lycra bra fabric with acid dye, you'll find that everything comes out about the same color; other fiber/dye combinations may produce more variations. Instructions for fabric dyeing are given in chapter 6.

Determining Cup Size

Difference between the full-bust measurement and band size	Cup size
No difference	AA
Up to 1 in.	A
2 in.	B
3 in.	C
4 in.	D
5 in.	DD (or E)
6 in.	DDD (or F)
7 in.	DDDD (or FF/G)

Test-Fitting the Cup

You need a second pair of hands to try the sample cup on your body before assembling the bra. For an underwire style, first pin the underwire to the lower edge of the sample cup.

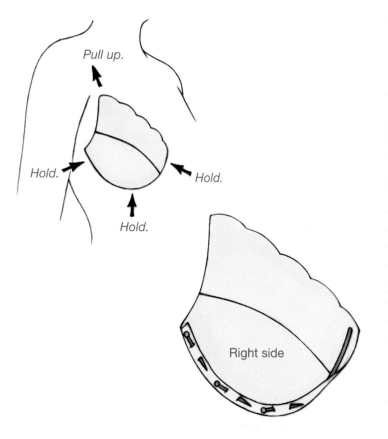

Pull up.

Hold.

Hold.

Hold.

Right side

sized). For example, if your ribcage measures 31 in., add 5 in. to get 36 in. as your bra-band size.

2 Measure around the fullest part of your bust, keeping the tape level and just tight enough to keep it from slipping. The difference between this full-bust measurement and the band size determines your cup size. See the chart at left to convert this number into a traditional bra cup size from AA–DDDD.

The bra size you determine from these measurements is just a starting point. Variations in your body type can affect the result, so it's essential to make a fitting sample of the cup. I'll take a look at some of these factors and how they can affect your bra size in the sidebar on p. 101.

Test-fitting a sample cup

Now that you've got your measurements in hand, the next step is to construct a sample cup for a test-fit. It's best to correct the fit of the cup before working on the band, since the latter is an easy adjustment. Cut the cup out first, then check its fit by basting the cup sections together and "trying it on." You'll need two pairs of hands to hold the cup to your body at the side, the center front, directly under the bust, and pulled up where the strap attaches, as shown in the illustration at left. For an underwire style, first pin the wire into the cup by folding ⅜ in. around the wire to the outside and pinning parallel to the wire.

Adjusting the Pattern for Uneven Sides

If the bust is larger on one side, fit the sample cup on the larger side first, then alter to fit the smaller side. Make separate pattern pieces for the right and left sides and label them.

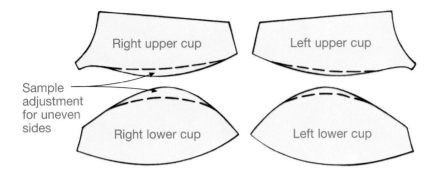

Sample adjustment for uneven sides

Right upper cup

Left upper cup

Right lower cup

Left lower cup

If the cup is too big, examine the fit. Does the breast fill the sides of the cup completely? If there are wrinkles of excess fabric across the cup seam but the diameter is right (allowing for seam allowances), pinch the excess fabric out along the seamline until the cup is smooth. Make a note on the pattern piece of how much was removed (i.e., ⅜ in. at bust point, tapering to nothing at the sides).

It's a good idea to fit both cups, since many women are larger on one side. If you find this is the case, start with the cup that fits the larger side, then alter it down to fit the smaller side. Make separate pattern pieces for right and left sides, if needed, and label them (see the illustration above).

If the cup is too small to cover the breast completely with some left over for seam allowances, you can try one of two solutions. The obvious choice is to cut a larger cup. But suppose the diameter of the cup seems okay, but the breast sticks out farther than average from the chest wall (the opposite of wide/shallow)? You'll need to add to the cup at the bust point, tapering down to

Adding to a Cup at the Front

If the diameter of a cup fits but the breast sticks out farther than average, add to the cup at the bust point, tapering to nothing at the sides.

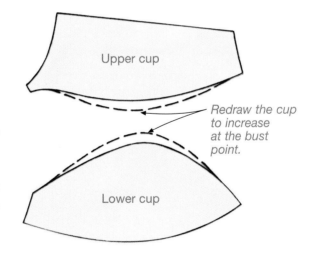

Upper cup

Redraw the cup to increase at the bust point.

Lower cup

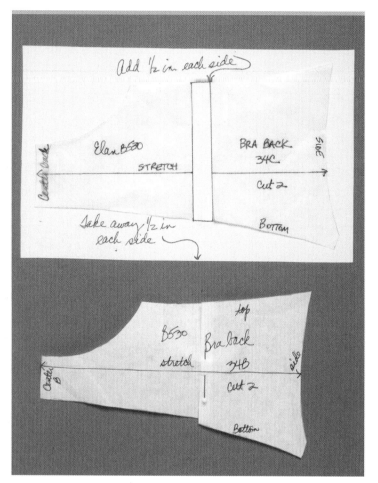

If the cup fits but the band is too large or too small, it's easier to adjust the band rather than switch to another size. Shown at the top, the band is slashed and spread to add ½ in. at each side of the bra; below, the band is folded to remove ½ in. at each side.

General Construction Techniques

Your bra pattern instructions will guide you through the construction for that specific style, but the following information provides an overview of the process, as well as some helpful tips for constructing a bra.

In general, bra seam allowances are ¼ in., and seams are sewn with a straight stitch or tiny zigzag. When using a straight stitch on knits, stretch the fabric slightly as you sew to build in some give. As always, test the stitch length/width and thread tension on scraps of your fabric before starting to sew. I've had great results with high-quality, long-staple polyester thread such as Mettler Metrosene and Gütermann and a size 70/10 Schmetz universal needle. Try whatever your sewing-machine manufacturer recommends that will give the result you want.

To help you visualize the steps, let's walk through the process of sewing a basic bra. While this sample may not be exactly like the bra you plan to make, the photos will more or less parallel the instructions in your pattern guidesheet. The bra shown here is a nylon/Lycra satin, back-closing style with a partial band and underwires using Élan pattern B530.

1 Begin by assembling the cups. Place the upper and lower cup pieces right sides together and pin at each end of the seam and at the marking. Instead of using a lot of pins, sew with the lower cup against the throat plate

nothing at the sides, as shown in the bottom illustration on p. 99.

Fitting the band

Once you get the cup right, fitting the band is easy. The simplest correction is to add to the band by slashing and spreading the pattern, as shown in the photo above, or fold out the excess to subtract a bit. Make any changes at the side of the band between the back strap and the cup. Remember to add or subtract only half of the total correction you need, since it's repeated on the left and right bands.

Common Fitting Challenges

Many factors contribute to proper fit in a bra. All of our bodies are slightly different in one way or another, and that's the beauty of making your own lingerie. Instead of trying to fit into just a few standard ready-to-wear sizes, sewing your own gives you the opportunity to fine-tune the fit so it's right for your unique body. Here are some common fitting problems and their solutions:

❏ **If you have a wide back:** You may need a smaller cup size than the measurements indicate. For example, if your measurements suggest that you're a size 36C but you have a wide back, you may want to start with a size 36B.

❏ **If you have a wide, shallow bust:** If your bust starts at your side seam but doesn't extend very far from your chest wall (a common fitting challenge), you'll need to start with a larger cup size to accommodate the width of the breast, then take the excess fullness out of the cup at the point.

❏ **If the bra rides up in back:** Since the bra band should support most of the bust's weight, it should be comfortably snug around the body and straight across the back or dip slightly lower in back. If the band rides up in back, the weight of the bust is relying too heavily on the straps, which can cause the straps to dig into the shoulders. If you're sure the cups fit correctly, then either the band needs to be tighter or it needs to be wider from top to bottom.

❏ **If the bra band rolls:** On some full-figured women, a wide bra band tends to roll up. To correct this problem, use wide, firm elastic at the band's lower edge or sew casing strips at the sides, inserting flexible boning before adding the elastic, to provide more structure.

STEP 2

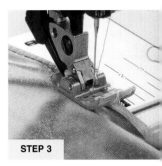

STEP 3

Step 2: To finish the center-cup seam, press it to one side and topstitch ⅛ in. away, through all layers.

Step 3: Dyed-to-match, fold-over elastic makes a clean finish at the upper bra-cup edge. Fold the elastic to enclose the edge and sew using a multiple zigzag stitch, stretching the elastic slightly.

and stop often with the needle down to reposition the edges, then continue sewing.

2 To finish the seam, press it to one side—down for a single-layer lower cup or up for a double one. A tailor's ham makes it easy to press a smooth curve. Topstitch ⅛ in. from the seam through the seam allowances. For a heavier fabric, press the seam allowances open and topstitch on each side. Trim close to the stitching.

3 Finish the upper edge of the bra cup with lace, fold-over elastic, or a facing.

STEP 4

STEPS 5–7

STEP 8

STEP 9

STEP 10

4 Join the cups with the center-front piece, aligning the edges carefully. Backstitch at the begining and end. For a front-hook bra, sew the hook assembly and attach it to the cups.

5 Before measuring and cutting the plush elastic, stretch it a few times to keep it from "growing" as you stitch. Measure the lower edge of the bra band, and cut elastic to 80 percent of that length. Then mark the elastic and bra band in quarters: Fold the piece in half and pin at the center, then fold the ends to the center and pin at each fold.

6 Apply elastic to the right side of the band with the plush side facing up and the picot edge pointing away from the fabric edge. Matching marks on the elastic and band, use a narrow zigzag to stitch along the edge of the elastic near the picots, stretching the elastic to fit. Trim the fabric close to the stitching.

7 Turn the elastic to the inside so the fuzzy side will be next to the body and the picots show at the edge. Sew again along the straight edge of the elastic using a narrow zigzag, or stitch down the center using a wide, multiple zigzag stitch.

8 Join the band to the cup, matching edges carefully. Continue stitching around the cup to the bottom of the center-front piece.

9 Add the channeling. With the cup on the bottom, right side up, and with

tip. . .

For set-in cups in a nonunderwire style, use a folded strip of tricot to finish the seam where the cup joins the band. On underwire styles, the channeling that holds the wire also finishes the seam.

the center front and bra back folded back on top, align the stitching on the channeling with the stitching on the cup. Stitch close to the inner edge of the channeling, pulling the channeling snug as you sew, which helps it roll to the inside. Trim the ends, leaving a $\frac{1}{2}$-in. tail at each end.

10 Turn and press the channeling to the inside and topstitch close to both long edges of channeling, if desired, to prevent it from rolling to the outside.

11 Cut, mark in quarters, and use the same application method given in steps 5 and 6 to sew plush elastic to the upper edge of the band and the armhole of the cup, allowing 1 in. of elastic to extend beyond the top of the cup.

12 To add the straps, fold the elastic at the top of the cup through a ring and stitch securely. Assemble the straps as shown in the illustration on p. 58, then sew the end of the strap elastic to the upper edge of the bra back.

13 Sew on the back bra closure, and finish the raw edges, if needed.

14 Insert the underwires by sliding the wire into the channeling, making sure it's inside the channeling, not

STEP 12

STEP 14

under it, as shown in the photo on p. 97. When fully inserted, underwires should be at least ½ in. to ¾ in. shorter than the finished channeling to allow the wire to move freely without working through the bra. If the underwire fits too tightly, you'll need to shorten it (see the tip at right).

15 Always check that the wire is out of the way when sewing the channeling closed because stitching over the wire may result in the needle breaking and

see the photo on p. 97

> **tip...**
>
> *Depending on your bra style and the pattern company, the straps may be added at several points during the bra construction, so check your instruction sheet. Some patterns direct you to baste straps to the back before applying the upper edge elastic.*

possible eye injury. On the right side, sew a line of very narrow satin stitches at the center front of the upper cup, closing the channeling. Trim the end even with the upper edge.

Converting a Bra Pattern to a Racer or V-Back

Appearing frequently in ready-to-wear, racer- and V-back bras are comfortable styles to wear and have a clean, sporty look. They offer the added advantage of cooperating when worn under T-shirts and tanks with scooped back armholes—because of their placement, the straps don't show. Especially if you have a small frame or have narrow or sloping shoulders (with the accompanying annoyance of bra straps that frequently slip off), you may want to consider

> **tip...**
>
> *There are two ways you can shorten an underwire and create a secure, finished end. Either pull off the plastic tip, cut the wire with wire cutters, then put the tip back on, or dip the cut end in a steel epoxy such as J-B Weld, available at hardware and auto-supply stores, to make a new, rounded tip that won't poke through the channeling.*

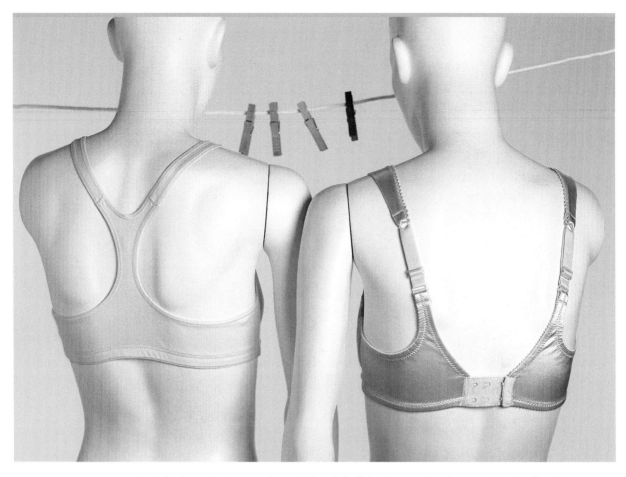

Both the front-closing racer-back (left) and the V-back bra styles give a comfortable fit with straps that stay put on the shoulders. It's easy to adapt a regular bra pattern to create either style.

adapting your bra pattern to a neat racer- or V-back style.

It's a fairly easy job to convert your pattern. For either of these bra styles, you can adjust the dimensions to suit your personal preferences, but the original band length should not be altered if you want to maintain the same fit.

To redraw the pattern, you'll need a few basic patternmaking tools:

❏ a see-through ruler
❏ pattern-tracing paper
❏ a dressmaker's (or French) curve

❏ ½ yd. more elastic than the pattern specifies

Converting to a racer back

Use the racer-back conversion when you're working with a front-closing bra pattern. The straps attach to the bra between the shoulder blades, which makes the style extremely comfortable to wear.

1 On a sheet of paper, lightly trace the back bra-band pattern piece. Continue the center-back line up 8 in.

from the bottom of the band, as shown in the top illustration. Make a mark 7 in. up from the bottom and another ⅜ in. above the first mark.

2 Using a ruler, draw lines through the marks at right angles from the center-back line. From the point where the lower line crosses the center back, mark 1¾ in. in both directions.

3 Using the curve, draw a U-shaped line from the mark on the center-back line through the second mark, ending at the top line. Draw another line 1¼ in. from this point to the lower line, as shown in the center illustration.

4 Use the curve again to draw a curved line from the end of the 1¼-in. line down to blend with the upper edge of the back bra band (see the bottom illustration).

Once you've altered the pattern, cut the new pattern piece on the fold with the greater stretch running around the body. Apply elastic to the lower edge of the band before sewing the band to the cups. After the cups are attached, apply elastic to the upper edges. If needed, shorten the straps before attaching them to the band.

Converting to a V-back

A V-back bra style is an ingenious design that adapts the successful features of a racer-back style to one that works on a back-closing bra. It offers

Converting to a Racer Back

Trace a back bra-band pattern piece and continue the center-back line up 8 in. from the bottom. Mark 7 in. from the bottom and ⅜ in. above the first mark. Draw lines through the marks at right angles from the center-back line and mark 1¾ in. in both directions from the intersection of the lower line.

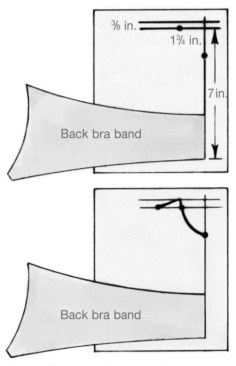

Draw a U-shaped line from the mark on the center-back line through the second mark to the top line. Draw a line 1¼ in. from this point to the lower line.

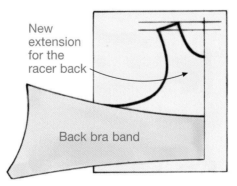

Draw a curved line from the end of the 1¼-in. line to the upper edge of the back bra band.

Adding Support for a Large Bust

For a full-busted figure, you may find that many of the fabrics and regular bra construction techniques simply do not provide enough support. The best support starts with choosing the right style—a full-band bra with set-in, underwired cups, wide elastic around the lower edge, and a wide band made of firm stretch fabric such as Power Net.

While many lightweight knits make a nice-looking bra, they may require added support for a larger bust. One solution is to cut two layers of fabric for the cup with the direction of greater stretch running perpendicular to each other and baste them together. For easier handling, glue-baste the layers using a product such as Insta-Pin (Simplicity) or Glue Pin (Sullivans) or a regular glue stick. Do this by placing one layer wrong side up and dotting glue around the edges, then covering with the second layer right side up. Press with a warm iron.

Create even more support by fusing a tricot interfacing such as Stacy Easy-Knit inside one or both layers of the cup, with the direction of greater stretch running in the same direction as the piece you're fusing to. Choose a fusible close to the color of your fabric, dye them together (see pp. 112–115 on dyeing lingerie), or use beige or nude.

In nonunderwire styles, you can also add support by sewing a half-moon insert to the side of each cup at an angle to push the bust upward and inward. Make the inserts from firm interfacing or fleece fused between two layers of lightweight fabric like tricot. Or you can reinforce the entire lower cup in the same way.

the same comfort with the closure sewn between close-set straps.

1 Lightly trace the back bra-band pattern piece. Add ⅜ in. to the center back, and continue the center-back line up 8 in. from the bottom of the band. Mark 7 in. up from the bottom.

2 Using a ruler, draw a line through the mark at a right angle from the center-back line. Make two marks on this line, one at 1¼ in. and one at 2½ in. from the center-back line, as shown in the top illustration on the facing page.

3 Using a curve, draw a slight curve from the 1¼-in. mark down to the top of the band at the center back. Draw a curve from the 2½-in. mark to blend with the upper edge of the bra band, as shown in the bottom illustration on the facing page.

Converting to a V-Back

Trace the back bra-band pattern. Add ⅜ in. at the center back and continue the center-back line up 8 in. from the bottom. Mark 7 in. up from the bottom.

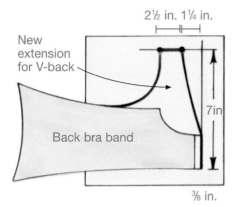

New extension for V-back

2½ in. 1¼ in.

7 in.

Back bra band

⅜ in.

Draw a line through the mark at a right angle from the center-back line. Make two marks on this line, one at 1¼ in. and one at 2½ in. from the center-back line.

Draw a slight curve from the 1¼-in. mark down to the top of the band at the center back. Draw a curve from the 2½-in. mark to the upper edge of the bra band.

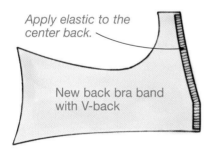

Apply elastic to the center back.

New back bra band with V-back

When cutting out the pattern, cut two back bra bands (left and right) with the greater stretch running around the body. Apply elastic to the bottom of the bra band, then apply elastic to the slight curve and edge of center back in one piece, curving the elastic as needed. Enclose the center-back elastic with the back hook closure and stitch to secure.

Adding a Pocket for a Mastectomy Prosthesis

It's not difficult to convert an existing bra or one you plan to sew to hold a mastectomy prosthesis. However, the ideal bra to wear after a mastectomy is a very individual decision, and what you want will depend on the type and location of the surgery, the healing time, and the shape of the prosthesis.

To add a soft pocket to an existing bra:

1 Using the paper-and-pin method, make a pattern from the cup as it lies flat on a table. To do this, tape two layers of pattern-tracing paper over foam-core or cardboard. Tape the bra to the paper, as shown in the top left illustration on p. 108, smoothing the armhole and upper and lower cup edges as much as possible.

2 Starting at the strap, use a pin to poke holes through the bra and onto the pattern paper along the following lines: along the edge of the upper cup; the seamline where the cup joins the center front; the curved lower edge at the bottom of the cup; the side seamline where the cup joins the

Adding a Pocket for a Mastectomy Prosthesis

It's easy to add a soft pocket to a purchased bra's inner cup.

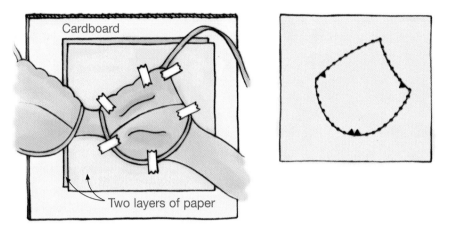

Tape two layers of paper over cardboard. Tape the bra to the paper, smoothing the armhole, upper, and lower cup edges as much as possible. Use a pin to poke holes along the edge all around the cup. Remove the bra and draw along the holes on both layers. Make notches on both layers for aligning.

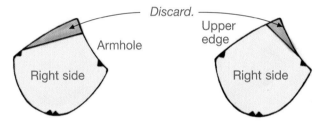

To create an opening to insert the prosthesis, draw a line on one layer from the armhole diagonally to the top edge of the upper cup for an open edge. On the other layer, draw a line from the upper cup diagonally down to the armhole. This is the open edge for the second layer.

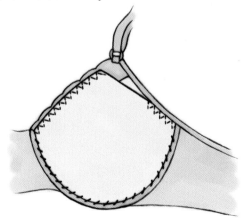

A cup with the completed pocket and top opening

band; and along the armhole edge back up to the strap.

3 Remove the bra and trace around the holes in the pattern paper with a pencil, smoothing small inaccuracies, on both layers. (A French or dressmaker's curve can help.) Make notch marks on both layers to make aligning the layers easier (see the top right illustration on the facing page).

4 On one layer, draw a line from the armhole edge (about 1 in. from the strap, depending on cup style/size) diagonally to the top edge of the upper cup (1 in. from the cup/center-front seam). This is the open top edge of the first layer (see the left center illustration on the facing page).

5 On the other layer, draw a line from the upper cup edge (1 in. down from the strap) diagonally down the armhole edge (1½ in. up from the side seam). This is the open edge of the second layer (see the right center illustration on the facing page). Label the right side, armhole, and upper edges on each piece.

6 Cut each piece from soft, lightweight cotton knit, then finish the opening edges with a small zigzag, a serged edge, narrow stretch lace, or fold it under and stitch. Since the fabric doesn't ravel, you just want to stabilize the edge without adding bulk.

7 Baste the two layers together, leaving the finished edges open. Pin the pocket into the cup and stitch it in place, zigzagging over the raw edges of the pocket (a three-step zigzag works well). If you're adding a pocket to an underwire bra, fold under the edge along the channeling and sew with a straight stitch at the very edge of the channeling, or hand-sew with a tiny whipstitch. Be sure you don't machine-stitch over the underwire.

CUSTOM DETAILS THAT MAKE IT YOUR OWN

While I'm planning a piece of lingerie that will fit and function beautifully, there's always a small voice in the back of my mind saying, "But isn't something missing?" Sure, it's nice if the garment fits and works well, but it can be a lot more fun when there's a creative element involved. It may be just a touch of embroidery, a special color, or even a scattering of beads.

This chapter includes a variety of quick takes on ways to alter a fabric and embellish a garment, including many of the techniques used to create the garments pictured in this book. Studying the fragile lingerie of New York designer Andra Gabrielle (see the sidebar "The Best of the Best" on pp. 128–130) will inspire you with its subtlety, balance, and perfect proportion. But in the end, the techniques you choose for your own garments will depend upon the look you want and your own personal style.

How can you hide this beautiful bra and panty? Sewn from lustrous silk/Lycra ottoman, the pieces are also comfortable because the Lycra allows the woven fabric to stretch. Embellished with hand-painting, they also include machine embroidery and delicate seed-bead edging.

A Menu of Finishing Touches

I find any project more satisfying when I can alter or play with it or embellish it to give it my mark. In truth, this is my favorite part—inventing the little touches that customize a ho-hum or less-than-interesting fabric, adding the "frosting" that can make the piece so appealing. Just a few beautiful elements can make your garment not only more pleasurable to wear but also more fun to sew. And a little extra time spent on the right details can lift your creation from the ordinary to the delicious. Some of my favorites include:

Fabric dye or textile paint. If you can't find a fabric that's just what you want, one solution is to use fabric dye or textile paint to customize a fabric. Both dyes and paints are easy to use and can dramatically change a fabric's look or color. You can saturate a nylon/spandex satin bra and panty with a blast of intense color. Or you can add stripes or prints to express your whimsy.

Appliqué. Appliqué offers a smooth way to integrate another fabric or color into a simply styled garment. I'll show you how to use appliqué to finish a facing that lies on the outside of a garment.

Embroidery and beading. Small doses of these elements can provide the "frosting" on a special bra, gown, or robe. A fine sprinkling of tiny beads combined with the subtle sheen of rayon machine-embroidery can add rich texture to a luxury garment.

Silk ribbon. Silk ribbon is amazingly versatile as a tool for embellishment. From a simple, polished bound edge to a cluster of embroidered flowers, silk ribbon combines its luster with that of silk fabric to create a beautiful effect.

Before beginning any dyeing project, it's a good idea to prewash the fabric to remove any dye-resistant finishes.

When you add the details that make a garment special, you may find yourself smiling every time you wear it. For me, this subtle use of embellishment is what makes perfect lingerie so much fun to sew. In the following pages, you'll find examples of these ideas and more.

Fabric Dyes and Textile Paints

So many wonderful choices abound in the world of fabric dye and paint. It's fun to experiment with all the options, but it's perhaps a more reasonable idea to play with one at a time until you're comfortable with the technique.

The difference between dye and paint is that fabric dye chemically bonds with the fiber itself, while paint lies on top of the fabric. Either dye or paint can be used to permanently change the solid color of a fabric or to create a design on fabric. Which product to use depends on the look you want and the fiber content of your fabric. Since some dyes are compatible with certain fabrics and not with others, you need to match the dye with the fiber. Textile paints, on the other hand, can be used on most fabrics. In this chapter, I'll explain a few dye and paint methods used to create garments you see in this book.

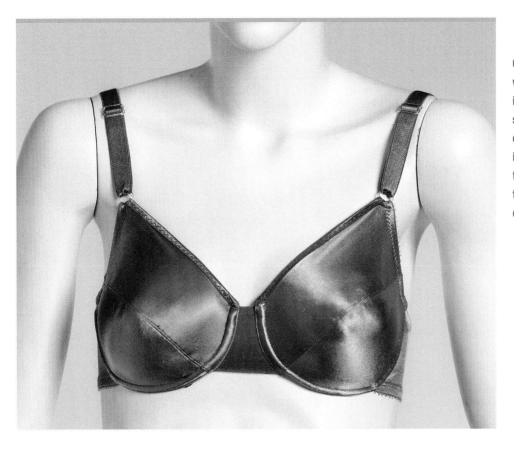

Constructed with plain white fabric and findings, this nylon/Lycra satin bra got a quick dye bath in the washing machine to create the luscious color. So that's why all the elastics match!

Using fabric dye for solid colors

In spite of the wide selection of fabrics available, it can still be challenging to find the color you have in mind in the fabric you want. Especially when it comes to sewing bras, it can be impossible to locate all the findings and elastics in that same color (unless what you want is black or white!). One easy way to solve this dilemma is to begin with white fabric and findings, and dye the completed garments the color you want, as taught by Cindy Elam of Élan Patterns. Or you can dye the fabric yardage and findings before assembling the garment.

Using Jacquard acid dyes, I've had beautiful results dyeing nylon and silk fabrics, as well as many types of elastic, bra findings, and laces. There are two methods to choose from, depending on the depth of color you want: the washing-machine method and the stove-top method. It's easiest to dye your garments or fabrics in a washing machine, but dyeing in a pot on the stove produces a richer dark color, if that's what you're after.

Jacquard acid dye is available in many art-supply stores that carry dyes and silk painting accessories, as well as

tip. . .

If you'd like to use a similar dyeing technique on other fibers such as cotton or rayon along with elastic and findings, experiment with a combination dye such as Rit, which is available in grocery, hardware, and craft stores.

by mail (see Resources on p. 135). Before starting to dye, always read the instruction sheet for safety warnings. Jacquard acid dyes are nontoxic when used properly, but it's always best to use common sense and good housekeeping when handling any dye or chemical. This means wear gloves, don't inhale the powder, and don't reuse the same utensils for cooking.

Washing-machine method Water temperature, dye concentration, and length of time all affect the depth of color. In other words, hotter water, more dye, and longer dyeing time will result in a deeper color. For deep colors, use just enough very hot water to allow the fabric to move freely in the tub. To give the dye more time, you can run the washer through two or three wash cycles, resetting the machine before it starts to drain. (I set a kitchen timer to remind myself when to reset the machine.)

After completing the dye process, clean the washer by running it through a cycle with bleach before doing laundry as usual. If you're dyeing small findings and elastic before they're sewn into a garment, place the pieces in a mesh bag to prevent loss or tangling.

To use the washing-machine method, you'll need:

❏ a mesh bag for findings and elastics (needed only for dyeing loose pieces)
❏ individual dye packet (0.9 grams)
❏ ½ cup white vinegar to set the dye

1 Turn your water heater as hot as it will go for 30 minutes, then set your washer for hot wash/cold rinse and the lowest water level. Turn it on.

2 When the washer has filled, stop it and add the dye carefully. Agitate for six minutes to dissolve the dye.

3 Add the garment or fabric and findings.

4 Agitate for two minutes, then add vinegar (do not pour it directly on the fabric).

5 Let the machine run through the cycle, or reset it and agitate longer.

6 When finished, wash the fabric and findings in cool water and liquid soap.

Stove-top method If you want a deeper, dark color, use this method because the stove allows you to increase the temperature of the dye bath.

To use the stove-top method, you'll need:

❏ a large enamel or stainless-steel pot
❏ dye packet (0.9 grams)
❏ ¼ cup white vinegar
❏ a dye-resistant tool such as a long, stainless-steel spoon for stirring
❏ a candy thermometer, if desired

1 In a quart container, add the dye to one quart of very hot water from the tap and stir until dissolved.

2 Fill the large pot with enough hot water for the fabric to "swim" freely.

Add the dye solution and vinegar, stir, then add the fabric and findings. If needed, add additional water.

3 Raise the temperature to 180°F, using a candy thermometer or just watching for bubbles around the edges. Stir frequently for half an hour.

4 Remove the fabric and findings, and wash them in cool water and liquid soap.

Using textile paint to create solid colors

Textile paints are another way to achieve interesting color effects on fabric. Although they're normally used for printing, stamping, or freehand drawing, I decided to use textile paint to change the entire color of a fabric. An advantage of using textile paint is that it can give quicker, more immediate results than dye, and it's possible to play with interesting variegated effects.

For the charcoal-colored bra and panty shown in the photo on p. 111, I found a wonderful fabric—a woven silk/spandex ottoman—but in the wrong color. I decided to transform the predictable cream color to a rich, heathery charcoal gray so I could add the black embroidery and seed beads I wanted. (Élan pattern B530 provided the smooth, sleek styling and the option for a wider, self-fabric strap for comfort.)

After experimenting on samples using both dye and watered-down black and silver fabric paints, I preferred the variegated, taupe-gray effect I got with Deka black fabric paint diluted with lots of water. The diluted paint gave the fabric an interesting, heathered effect that almost looks marbleized.

To color the fabric, I first cut out the bra and panty sections, then immersed the pieces in the watered-down paint mixture for a few minutes. When the color seemed fairly even and deep enough (it lightens as it dries), I spread the pieces face up on a towel and left them to dry. Working with small pieces makes it easy to immerse them and control the color effect. With a larger piece of fabric, you might just want to dribble watered-down paint evenly all over the fabric for a variegated look. After allowing the pieces to dry, I ironed them on the wrong side to permanently set the color before assembling the garments.

Creating Designs with Dye

To create a stripe or print on your fabric, there are a number of different dye or textile paint products to choose from. I enjoy using a unique product called Inkodye (see Resources on p. 135), a nontoxic vat dye (the most permanent type of dye) that produces beautiful colors, creates no stiffness on the fabric, and cleans up with water. The unusual thing about Inkodye is that it's photosensitive; it looks nearly clear when applied to the fabric but develops and becomes permanent upon exposure to bright sunlight, so it requires no further setting.

You can spray or splatter with Inkodye or use stencils, a brush, or a silkscreen to apply it. I'll show you two very different ways I've used this unique dye: to create simple stripes on a cotton chenille fabric and to print softly col-

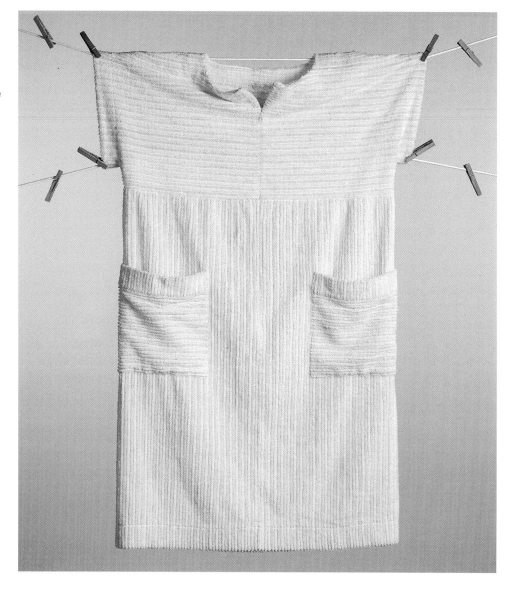

On a hot summer day, try a cool, cotton chenille robe. An easy dye process transformed the white fabric with furry woven ribs into fresh blue and white stripes.

ored leaf designs on cotton knit. As always (especially when trying something new), I suggest practicing on swatches of fabric until you're happy with the color and feel confident about the finished results. Then take a deep breath and dive in!

Watercolor Stripes

Maybe I'm stubborn (hah!), but once I got the idea into my head that I wanted soft, blue-and-white-striped cotton che-

nille for a summer robe, it was hard for me to accept that I couldn't find that fabric. Luckily, I located solid-white cotton chenille with furry lengthwise ribs and realized that I could easily add pale blue stripes with the help of a metal-tip squeeze bottle and Inkodye.

Inkodye can be applied to either wet or dry fabric, but because I wanted soft, watery-looking stripes with softly blurred edges, I wet the fabric first and spun it in the washer to remove excess water. Diluting blue Inkodye with lots of water gave me the pale blue shade that I used to lightly color every other furry rib woven into the chenille. To do this, I spread the fabric out flat (working on the clean kitchen floor gave me enough room to avoid bunching) and ran the bottle down each row at an even speed, as shown in the photo at right.

Although this is an easy and mindless process, it took me several hours to color enough fabric to make the robe, working at my slow, careful speed. Because the dye is so diluted, the resulting color is variegated, similar to pale, faded denim. To make the color even lighter, I allowed the fabric to dry before placing it in the sun. If you want brighter colors, you can use less water and expose the fabric to sun while the Inkodye application is still wet. To learn how much color to use for the effect you want, mix colors and test them on samples, then develop the samples in the sun.

Leaf printing

While stripes are an easy way to become familiar with Inkodye, ideas for more interesting designs can come from just about anywhere and can be as simple or as complex as you like. I remember looking through a copy of Garnet Hill, a natural-fiber mail-order catalog, and seeing a sheer cotton voile curtain with softly colored printed leaves strewn randomly about. Right away I could visualize the same type of print on a short summer gown and kimono.

To apply an Inkodye/water mixture, fill a metal-tip squeeze bottle with the dye solution and run the tip down every other woven chenille stripe. Working on wet fabric gives a soft, watercolor look.

tip. . .

Undiluted Inkodye colors are very strong, so dilute each color or color mixture with water if you want to make the dye thinner and more fluid (as needed for the stripes). You can also dilute it with clear Inkodye to lighten the color without changing the consistency (as needed for leaf printing).

The coolest summer gown of glossy cotton knit gets a custom print design using real leaves and Inkodye.

So I set to work. For the fabric, I chose a glossy, Austrian cotton knit because it's soft, beautiful, and durable. Then I collected a ziplock bag of 1-in.- to 2-in.-long leaves on a trip to Florida (there aren't many leaves to print with in Boston, I realized, during the winter). Because I wanted to position the leaf prints on the gown and robe, I cut out

tip. . .

If you're collecting leaves up to two weeks ahead of time, seal them in a Ziplock bag and refrigerate until you're ready to print. Some sturdy leaves can even be frozen and thawed for repeated use.

the garments before printing, but you could also print on the yardage before cutting.

Making the leaf prints By applying two or three colors of Inkodye to different areas of a leaf, it's possible to create some lovely shaded variations of color within a single leaf print. First, I mixed a few medium-light colors that I wanted to use on my gown and robe in green, yellow, persimmon, and violet. To mix a medium-light color, try four brushfuls of clear to half of a brushful of colored dye; mix them in a small jar or dish like a shot glass or on a palette.

For distinct areas of color, brush a small amount of each color on different areas of a leaf without mixing them. Or you can blend a new color right on the leaf. You can't see the final colors until the fabric develops in the sun, so making samples and taking notes is essential (unless you just want to wing it!).

To print with leaves, you'll need:

❏ pieces of cardboard large enough to hold your garment sections (I sliced open two large cardboard boxes)
❏ Inkodye colors, mixed to create the colors you want
❏ fresh leaves in a variety of shapes
❏ a paintbrush or two

❏ small jars or bowls for mixing dyes and a bowl for water
❏ clean scrap paper, cut in pieces to cover a leaf
❏ a plastic or metal tray or other surface for applying dye
❏ paper towels for drying leaves and the surface

1 Tape the garment pieces to the cardboard using masking tape. (You don't have to print all the pieces at once.) Lay out the leaves on the garment to plan a design.

2 One at a time, brush small amounts of two or three colors of dye onto different areas of the veined side of a leaf. The underside of the leaf will give a more detailed print.

3 Reverse the coated leaf onto the fabric. Cover with scrap paper and press in place, then remove the paper and leaf.

4 Repeat on other areas of the piece. Rinse the leaf in clean water and dry gently with a paper towel before applying a different color.

5 When the garment piece is covered with prints to your liking, place the cardboard in the sun to develop the colors. In bright sun, 15 to 30 minutes is long enough; on a partly cloudy day, the colors may take an hour or more to develop.

If you're not sure about the design (which is understandable since you can't

Step 2: Mix several colors of Inkodye, then brush a small amount of two or three colors on the underside of a leaf. Placing the colors on separate areas of the leaf will create a multicolored print.

Step 3: To print, press the coated leaf onto the fabric using a square of clean paper.

STEP 2

STEP 3

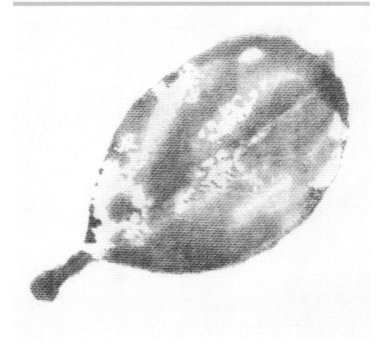

Using several different leaf shapes and three or four colors of your choice will result in a varied group of soft, natural prints.

really see where you put the colors), it's a good idea to develop what you've printed so far. Then it's easy to see where else you want to add prints.

Although I planned the gown and kimono shown in the photo on p. 110 as a matching set, it was more interesting to vary the design between pieces for a custom look. I used slightly smaller, more closely spaced leaf prints on the gown and larger leaves with wider spacing in the same colors on the kimono. After the fabric is printed, the pieces are quick and easy to sew. Finally, wash the completed pieces to remove any dye residue and resulting stiffness.

Experimenting with Textile Paints

If you'd like to try using textile paints for printing, stamping, or painting, there are many interesting paints available such as Deka Permanent Fabric Paint, Setacolor by Pebeo, and Versatex Textile Paint. Some are sheer, others are opaque, and still others have metallic or pearlized effects, and the colors are dense, brilliant, and permanent. In general, for printing and stamping, you don't add water to the paint because you want it to have a thick consistency on your stamp or brush; some paints are thicker than others. For best results, cover your work surface with cardboard to protect it, then tape the fabric smoothly over that.

Rubber stamps work well as applicators for textile paint if the stamp's design grooves are deep and well defined (for a clean print, avoid getting paint into the grooves or spaces). Apply the paint evenly using a brush, then press the stamp onto the fabric. Experiment first on scrap fabric to determine the colors and design that you want. You can use purchased stamps, or you can cut your own designs from rubber erasers using an X-Acto knife. You could also try printing with objects found around your house, like the end of a thread spool, the prongs of a plastic fork, an unfolded paper clip, or a folded piece of cardboard. Try pasta, even, or leaves. You'll be surprised at the interesting images you can get.

After printing, allow the paint to dry completely. Iron the fabric on the wrong side for a couple of minutes to set the color so it will stand up to light and washing, following the instructions on your paint jar. Then wash and dry the fabric to remove any excess paint and soften the fabric.

Appliqué

Appliqué is one way to smoothly integrate additional fabrics and colors into a garment. You can appliqué a little or a lot, in solid colors or prints of any shape you want, or even build a whole new fabric. For my soft, washed linen pajamas pictured on p. 4, I decided to use appliqué in a minimal way, adding just a single additional color to a solid-color garment in the form of a contrasting facing.

Appliqué is not only a great way to enhance the look of a garment but also can be functional. The pale blue linen appliqué along the edges of the front doubles as the garment's facing, which is turned to the outside (instead of hiding on the inside as facings typically do) and finished with smooth satin stitching along the curved edges.

Breezy appliqué that doubles as a facing

To create the two-tone, appliquéd pajama fronts, I used a curvy, scalloped design that has a watery feel and made

For whimsical appliquéd edges: A pale blue facing sewn and turned to the outside of the simple handkerchief-linen pajama shirt creates an opportunity for embellishment. Each scallop on the vertical front makes a perfect spot for a button and buttonhole.

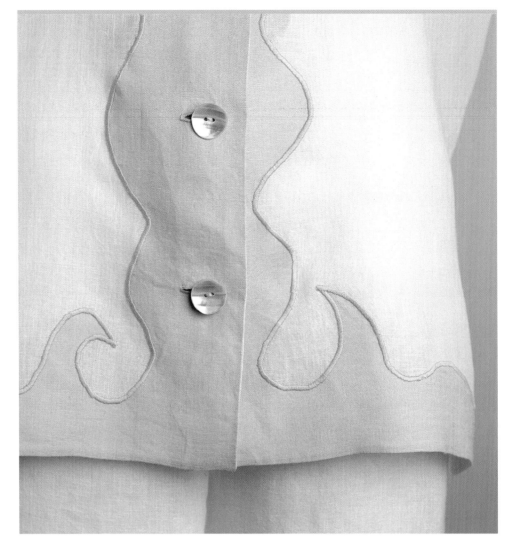

the two sides slightly different. You can use whatever design comes to mind— big zigzags, smooth, symmetrical curves, or elaborate scrollwork, depending on the look you want and the amount of time you'd like to spend stitching.

To use this technique, you'll need a few basic tools:

❏ spray starch
❏ tearaway stabilizer such as Stitch & Ditch by ThreadPRO

❏ for satin stitching, cotton thread such as Mettler 50/3 silk-finish cotton embroidery thread
❏ paper for practicing the appliqué shape

1 Begin by cutting out the garment pieces, including blocks for the left and right facings that are cut accurately at the neck, front, and lower edges but are wide enough for you to create the design you want for the appliqué.

2 Before joining the pj front and facing, apply several light coats of spray starch to each. To prevent sticking, allow the starch to soak in, then iron to give the shirt fronts and appliqué pieces a crisp finish.

3 Place the right side of the facing to the wrong side of the front and pin. Sew around the neck, center front, hem, and side-vent edges. Trim the seam allowances, clip corners, and turn the facing to the outside, creating crisp corners. Press.

4 On the facing, use a pencil, chalk, or marking pen to draw a curved line (or design of your choice) that will become its finished edge. I used soft, hand-drawn scallops, allowing a curve for every buttonhole plus a couple of soft, wavelike peaks, and added a little whimsy by making the left and right fronts slightly different.

5 Pin a layer of tearaway stabilizer on the wrong side of the front beneath the facing design lines to prevent the fabric from tunneling or buckling inside the satin stitching.

6 Using top thread that matches the facing fabric, sew a line of zigzag stitching (1.5mm wide and long) just inside the marked line, then carefully trim the facing along the line, just outside the stitching.

7 To finish the appliqué, satin-stitch along the edges using matching cotton thread; a stitch 3.5mm wide and 0.3mm long worked well for me. To follow curves smoothly, stop frequently with the needle in the fabric, lift the presser foot, and adjust the angle of stitching slightly before proceeding. I found that practicing on samples a few times immensely improved the look of my satin stitching.

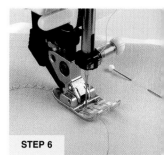

STEP 6

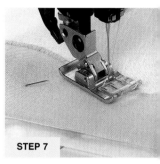

STEP 7

Step 6: Following the penciled line that defines the shape of the appliqué, use matching thread to zigzag neatly just inside that line.

Step 7: Use a wide, short zigzag to sew your smoothest, cleanest satin stitching to cover the previous stitching and the cut edge.

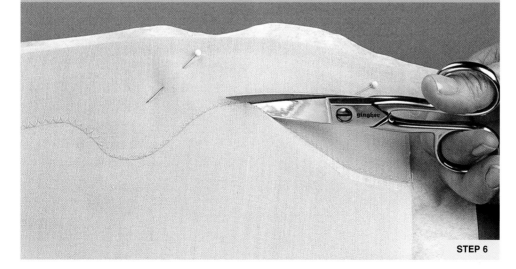

STEP 6

Step 6: Carefully trim the facing along the penciled line, just outside the stitching.

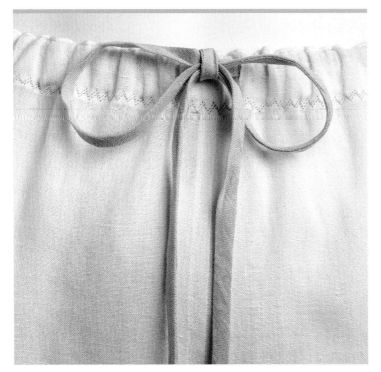

A skinny, bias-cut tie finishes the waist of the matching linen pants, offering another spot of pale blue to unify the pajama pieces.

Create a delicately textured line of stitching at the edge of a narrow hem using the tiniest twin needle and an elongated multiple zigzag stitch.

(Garment by Andra Gabrielle.)

When the appliqué is complete, you're ready to assemble the pajama top. I used flat-felled seams to construct strong, long lasting seams on the easy raveling linen, and finished the back neck with a bias strip of the blue linen to eliminate the need for a facing. Additional touches of blue on the pants unify the outfit (see the top photo at left). Wash the finished pieces to remove the spray starch.

Machine Embroidery and Beading

Many of today's sewing machines include beautiful embroidery stitches that you can use to embellish your lingerie. Embroidery can be very subtle when sewn in a thread that matches the color of the fabric or bolder when used as a contrast. You can also stitch a design twice in different colors for an interesting echo effect. Beads are another way to add texture and catch the light and are elegant when used in conjunction with embroidery. For a light lingerie feel, however, use them sparingly. I like to use seed beads to accent machine embroidery or to finish an edge.

Twin-needle stitching

Tiny twin-needle stitching, sewn with the narrowest 1.6/70 twin needle in either straight stitching or in an elongated multiple-zigzag stitch, is beautiful when used to anchor an edge or hem or to embellish a plain band of silk. Andra Gabrielle frequently uses this trim on her garments; actually, hers is often a custom serpentine stitch that she designed for her machine, but a three-step multiple-zigzag stitch also works well. On fine silk, use an extra-fine cotton machine-embroidery thread such as 50-weight DMC or Mettler 50/3 silk-finish cotton embroidery thread for the upper needles.

I borrowed this technique to add unifying touches of blue on my white linen pajama shirt and pants, using the three-step multiple-zigzag stitch with twin needles and the same blue cotton embroidery thread that edges the appliqué. This decorative stitching hems the shirt sleeves and pants and anchors the waistband casing (see p. 41).

Embroidery using preset stitches

To create texture and a delicate detail, try using tone-on-tone machine-embroidery stitches sewn in shiny rayon thread that matches your fabric. Many stitches on both mechanical and computerized sewing machines can be adapted for this type of embellishment.

For the charcoal-gray bra and panty shown on p. 111, I embellished the upper-cup sections and panty front before assembly with contrasting machine embroidery using black Sulky 40 rayon embroidery thread and a curved, scrolling stitch from my Pfaff 1473. A tearaway stabilizer (again, Stitch & Ditch by ThreadPRO) helped create more perfect stitches and prevent stretching.

After completing the black stitching, however, the embroidery looked a bit flat. On a sample, I repeated the design in salmon rayon thread (see the photo

Softly curving machine-embroidery scrollwork in two shades of shiny rayon thread embellishes the upper edge of an elegant special-occasion bra. For a fine finishing touch, add a sprinkling of seed beads and a tiny beaded picot edging.

above), slightly offsetting the second wave of embroidery so it looks like an echo or a reflection of the first. The second color brought the design to life, so I added salmon stitching to each of the garment sections. By hand, I sewed a few black seed beads randomly in the embroidered areas, skipping just a short distance from one bead to the next to avoid long threads on the back of the work. After the bra construction was complete, I beaded the upper-cup edges.

Beaded edges

The delicate, picot edging that embellishes the bra's upper cup is worked by hand in two steps using seed beads. Although the beading looks impressive,

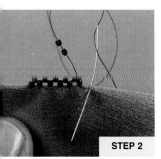

STEP 2

STEP 2

To work a beaded picot edging, pick up two beads and take a stitch from back to front through the top edge of the fabric. Insert the needle through the last bead added. Repeat these steps to the end of the row.

it's actually easy to do and works up quickly on such a small area. Practice on a sample first, and space your stitches evenly for the best result.

To embellish a piece of lingerie with embroidery or beading, you don't need to spend a lot of extra time. The smallest details can add immensely to the overall effect as well as pleasure in the wearing.

You'll need the following supplies:

❑ seed beads, size 11 (one tube is more than enough)
❑ nylon beading thread, Nymo size B
❑ a beading needle, size 12

1 Work from left to right with the edge facing away from you. With knotted thread, take a stitch in the fabric from back to front, hiding the knot, then backstitch to secure it. Pick up one bead, take a stitch from back to front, and insert the needle through the bead.

2 Next, pick up two beads, take a stitch from back to front, and insert the needle through the last bead added. Repeat to the end of the row.

Work a single continuous row of beading across the entire top edge of the bra from strap to strap, including the left cup, center section, and right

tip. . .

Always scrub your hands before starting to work with ribbon or beads; it's easy to transfer nearly invisible bits of dirt to the work that can never be washed away.

cup. Tie off the thread and bury the knot.

Silk Ribbon Details

Because of its lustrous thinness and extensive range of colors, silk ribbon serves many tasks beautifully. It's available in more than 200 colors, but it's also easy to create your own solid or subtly variegated colors using teas, dyes, or textile paints. The following elegant silk-ribbon cords, hems, and edge finishes are easy to sew and can add the perfect finish for delicate lingerie, with or without decorative embroidery and beading.

Flat-ribbon hems

After finishing the fabric's cut edge by using a serger or a maybelle hem (see "Narrow turned hems" on p. 40), simply lap a flat piece of ribbon over the fabric edge and sew at the top ribbon edge with a tiny zigzag. For more decoration, Andra sometimes adds a second band of narrower ribbon, in a matching or contrasting color, a short distance above the first, as shown in the photo on the facing page, or instead stitches along the center of the ribbon with a single-needle multiple-zigzag or other decorative stitch, using rayon thread in a matching shade. If desired, you can hand-sew tiny seed beads at regular intervals.

Silk-ribbon bound edges

You can create an elegant bound neckline or armhole edge on silk lingerie using silk ribbon, folded and sewn over the cut edge. This technique requires 7mm-wide ribbon, two passes of stitching, and a light touch. On the wrong

side, lay a length of ribbon along the cut edge, matching edges, and straight-stitch along the ribbon's inner edge. Trim the fabric's raw edge in half, then fold the ribbon over it to the right side. Anchor the second edge with a tiny zigzag stitch so that only the right-swinging stitches catch the edge of the ribbon.

Turned lace hems with silk ribbon

The turned lace hem discussed in chapter 3 makes a perfect finish when applying lace to an edge that ravels, such as the hems on the bias-cut yellow seersucker camisole and half-slip shown on p. 14. This technique gives a cleanly finished edge both inside and out. On those garments, I used narrow, crocheted cotton lace with a ladder top edge and laced silk ribbon through the ladder to anchor the top of the lace.

1 Start by placing the lace trim and edge wrong sides together, matching edges. Without stretching, sew ¼ in. from the trim's top edge using a narrow zigzag.

2 Turn the lace to the right side and press lightly, trimming the raw edge of the fabric if necessary. To enclose the fabric's raw edge and complete the design, thread a strand of 4mm silk ribbon on a chenille needle and sew with a running stitch in and out of the ladder edge of the lace. To arrange each ribbon stitch into a graceful curve, use a blunt tapestry needle to smooth the stitch as you pull it into place (see the top photo on p. 131). Avoid pulling the ribbon too tightly.

With pure silk ribbon, sew a line of easy running stitches to join the top edge of a turned cotton-lace hem. Use the flat side of the needle to "settle" each stitch so it lies flat.

THE BEST OF THE BEST

I f you'd like to sew exquisite silk lingerie for special occasions, there's no better source of inspiration than the lingerie garments created by Andra Gabrielle, a New York designer of exclusive lingerie and eveningwear.

Commanding top prices at stores such as Bergdorf Goodman and Barneys, these elegant, whisper-weight garments flatter every female form. Each piece is constructed in Andra's New York workrooms to her exacting standards, combining dozens of machine- and hand-sewn steps. My favorite peignoir sets are crafted from a single or double layer of French silk chiffon, weigh about as much as a dragonfly's wings, and feel just that light on the body; it's like wearing a second skin that enhances your own.

From studying Andra's lingerie, you can learn essential lessons about applying embellishment sparingly. But even so, don't forget—make samples first! Then you'll have those small successes to guide you.

Sew a simple little slip gown from two layers of the finest French silk chiffon, stencilled flowers, seed beads, and silk ribbon dyes make it irresistable.

(Garment by Andra Gabrielle.)

Irresistible Embellishments

In addition to Andra's sumptuous fabrics, the embellishments are the ingredients that make her gowns and robes so irresistible—the tiniest size 15 seed beads sprinkled lightly along an edge or at a flower's center, held in place with invisible hand stitches; a sheer, many-hued floral print hand-applied with stencils; or a trail of delicate machine embroidery in a shade that quietly matches the fabric. She uses thin, pure-silk ribbon in a multitude of creative ways, including folded and stitched to bind a cut edge, sewn along a hem, hand-sewn into lush, full-blown flowers, or twisted to form a slender slip strap or tie-cord that closes a robe. These delicate touches would almost look Victorian if the shapes weren't so clean, simple, and unfussy, and the details applied so sparingly. Even when all of these embellishments appear on a single, elegant garment, the result is still quietly understated.

A Close-Up Look

Several themes recur in Andra's work with breathtaking results. She frequently uses light, fragile fabrics;

subtle, usually tone-on-tone machine embroidery; and seed beads in size 13 and smaller. Silk ribbon appears in a variety of guises. And when laying out a garment, Andra places the fabric's selvages with great care to minimize bulk and eliminate unnecessary edge finishes in strategic spots on each style, often at very visible front edges or hems. Let's take a close-up look.

Gown and peignoir

The idea for this fragile robe's complex floral print came from the prints used on Japanese kimonos, which vary depending on the age and experience of the wearer. For a young woman's garment, the print is simple and in clear colors, symbolizing her limited life experience. The subtle, intricate print (hand-stenciled in soft shades) on the above robe, then, would be worn by an older woman with rich life experience.

Although the peignoir has a spare, simple shape with selvages placed at the center front and no side seams, this surface simplicity hides a multitude of delicious details. The selvages at the center front are turned under ¾ in. to form a narrow facing, then topstitched with an embroidery design in matching shiny rayon thread. An occasional tiny, hand-sewn seed bead accents the embroidery for the top few inches (see the detail on p. ii).

After stitching, the shoulder, sleeve, and armscye seams are wrapped in 7mm-wide silk ribbon and edgestitched for a smooth finish inside (on a sheer garment, there's nowhere to hide a less-than-perfect seam). Delicate printed flowers, as sheer as can be on French silk chiffon, float down the fronts, across the sleeves, and above the hem around the robe. Flowers at the hem are accented with a few seed beads (see the top photo on p. 130), while others receive tiny dabs of metallic paint.

A double-layer band of contrasting-color silk changé in slate blue and beige (woven from two colors, so it's iridescent) adds weight at the sleeve and lower hems, enhancing the robe's drape and movement. At the top of the hem bands, a single flat width of 7mm-wide silk ribbon in a light coffee shade bridges the color change from peach to blue, from garment to band, covering the join and held in place by the tiniest zigzag stitch along the upper edge. The deep V-neckline is finished with a simple ¼-in.-wide band of the chiffon, turned and sewn with the same tiny zigzag. At the bottom of the V, ties made from twisted silk ribbon and crys-

To create an exquisite gown and gossamer peignoir, start with clean lines and a soft, simple style that flatters every figure. Add the finest fabrics such as silk chiffon and satin, then layer on delicious details including hand-stenciling, silk ribbon, embroidery, and beads. (Garment by Andra Gabrielle.)

tal drops are anchored in place with a single embroidered flower in soft green and peach silk ribbon with beaded centers.

The matching slip gown is simple by comparison. Made from luminous pure-silk satin in a slightly brighter shade of peach, its color and sheen create a beautiful luster when softly filtered through the sheer chiffon of the robe. For this piece, Andra placed the selvages at the gown's center back. And because the selvage is so beautiful, (resembling tiny silk grosgrain ribbon with a single gold thread), she also used it to bind the V-front neckline edge, so that satin shows on the inside and the "grosgrain" lies on the right side. A tiny zigzag holds the binding in place.

At the gown's center front, three embroidered, silk-ribbon roses with clusters of crystal seed beads beautifully disguise the join in the binding. The necklines of the gown and robe differ so that the twisted ties of the robe fall just 2 in. below the roses, both framing and revealing them.

The gown's side seams are serged with cotton thread and the narrowest three-thread stitch. Raw edges at the

Top: It's all a matter of scale. Even when one corner of a hem reveals stenciled flowers, machine embroidery, silk ribbon, a contrasting border, and seed beads, the result is still quietly understated.

Bottom: The chiffon peignoir's twisted silk-ribbon ties reveal a trio of full-blown roses at the neck of the satin gown beneath. Note the details: embroidered flowers that anchor the ties, a crystal drop at each tie's end, and tiny seed beads scattered along the embroidered fronts.

(Garments by Andra Gabrielle.)

armholes and hem are turned under and topstitched with narrow, twin-needle embroidery; the center-back walking vent receives the same finish. For a final intriguing touch, the gown is cut a couple of inches longer than the robe, giving the ensemble a floaty, layered effect.

Two-layer slip gown

For the body-skimming slip gown, made from two layers of the thinnest, sheer French silk chiffon in ivory over pale blue, the effect is of a single, radiant fabric. Selvages form the hems of both layers, and the gowns are constructed separately with tiny serged side seams, then joined wrong sides together so the inside of the gown is completely finished.

Silk ribbon binds neck and armhole edges, enclosing the raw edges of both layers. Two bands of silk ribbon in blue and pale green embellish the hem of the ivory outer layer.

Simple, six-petal flowers stenciled in blue with green leaves embellish the ivory layer around the front neckline and below the low, curving back. The flower's centers are beaded with seed beads in unexpectedly bright pink, blue, yellow, and green. The simple blue bow that finishes the center-front neckline measures just ¾ in. from end to end.

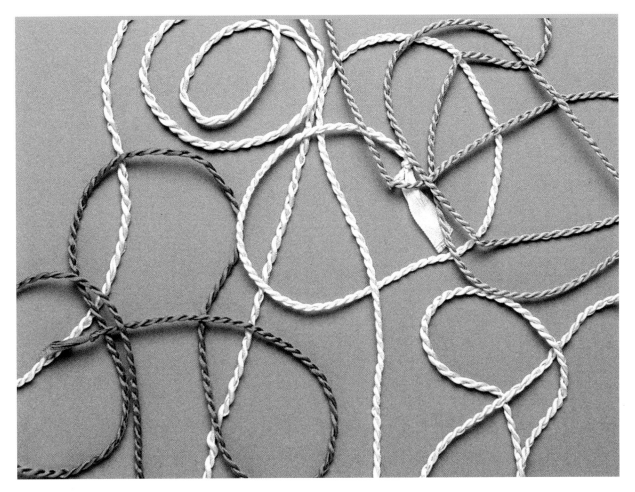

Twisted silk-ribbon cords in delicate colors stand ready to serve as ties or straps for a fragile silk gown.

Twisted cords from silk ribbon

When you see this elegant twisted cord, it's hard to believe how quickly it can be made from ordinary silk ribbon. Andra uses the cord for ties to close the front neckline of a peignoir, as well as for delicate straps on a bare-shouldered nightgown. My favorite is a low-backed, silk-chiffon ballet gown with straps that skim the shoulder blades and are anchored at the lower edges with simple, hand-embroidered silk-ribbon flowers.

To make the cord, start with 7mm-wide silk ribbon about four times the desired length of the finished tie or strap, cutting the ends on an angle to reduce raveling. A beautiful touch for a tie is to use a crystal drop or small antique button to serve as the weighted tip of the tie. To do this, first thread the end of the ribbon through the eye of the drop or button and slide it to the ribbon's center.

STEP 1

STEP 2

Step 1: With one end of the ribbon tied to the thread spindle, twist the other end until the curls become tight and the cord begins to curl back on itself.

Step 2: Holding the ribbon at the center, fold it in half and allow the halves to twist together.

1 Tie one end of the ribbon to the sewing-machine thread spindle and twist the other end repeatedly, spreading the curls evenly down the ribbon's length. Twist until the ribbon is tight and curling back on itself.

2 Fold the ribbon in half, and allow the two halves to twist together.

3 Open the ends (without releasing them), and add or remove curls until you're pleased with the result, then tie a knot with the two original ends.

Once you've made the cord, securely sew the twisted silk-ribbon tie or strap to the appropriate spot on the garment (at the neck edge for a robe's tie; at the upper V for a nightgown strap). Cover the join with a small leaf or flower hand-embroidered with silk ribbon, then wrap the ribbon around the cord to create a smooth join. Hand-sew to anchor the wrap.

Hand-embroidered details

To hide the join of a tie or strap or to lavishly embellish the center front of a gown, you can hand-embroider a leaf or flower detail as Andra does. At the join, a simple leaf may be formed from just a few stitches, while the flower details are often clusters of pale flowers with pearl or seed-bead accents. Let's take a look at both options.

Ribbon flowers detailed with silk floss and pearls A cluster of embroidered silk ribbon flowers can be the perfect finishing detail for a simple gown. When choosing ribbon colors, include a subtle variation to add depth, with the smaller flowers in a paler shade of the larger central one and using two shades of green for leaves (see the photo on the facing page). Lighter leaf colors help the leaves to recede behind the flowers.

To highlight the central flower, use a lustrous silk floss such as Ping Ling Silk from Kreinik, which is a six-ply continuous filament silk floss, in a color that blends with the ribbon. This will add a sheen at the petals' edges. A few tiny pearls and seed beads complete the flowers' centers.

Place the fabric in a hoop to stabilize the area, setting it tight enough to keep the cloth flat but not so tight that the hoop edges leave marks and using a hoop that leaves ample room around the design. Sew the petals first, using a long darner #5 or #7 needle with 7mm ribbon for the central flower.

To begin, knot the end of the ribbon, and bring the needle from below, near the center of the main flower. The ribbon will gather where it emerges and reenters the cloth; use your fingers and needle to control the shape of these folds. When you reinsert the ribbon into the cloth, lay the side of the needle under the forming petal and use it to control the ribbon's shape as you pull the excess through. You want the ribbon to form a lovely shape, so leave some fullness or pull it flat, depending on what pleases your eye. Practice a flower or two on a scrap of fabric with the exact materials to master the technique.

Hand-embroider a delicate arrangement of flowers using one simple stitch. By arranging the straight stitches gracefully, you can create petals and leaves and outline the flower in shinier silk floss. *(Garment by Andra Gabrielle.)*

Since the flower's center will be filled with pearls or beads, begin your stitches slightly off-center. The first petal determines the size of the flower, a circle twice the length of the petal plus the center. Sew each petal from the center to the outside, placing the first three stitches in the shape of a Y with a hole at the intersection. Then sew the remaining petals in the spaces between them; I used a total of nine petals for my central flower. When you finish the last petal, sew beneath one of the loops

on the back, then cut the ribbon, leaving ½ in. to anchor later.

Space the two side flowers a small distance away to leave room for leaves. Mine have five petals each in a lighter shade of 4mm ribbon. Next, add small leaves and buds using 4mm and 2mm ribbons. Complete the work on one side, then measure key placement points on the finished side and mark them on the other side so the design will be balanced. For example, measure the flowers from center to center, and check the

It's best to carefully handwash delicate, embellished silk gowns (of course, always prewash the fabric before cutting). When the piece is dry, press it lightly from the wrong side, placing beaded areas face down on a towel; avoid putting weight on embroidered flowers. From the right side, hold the iron above the flowers or other silk-ribbon embroidery, and steam thoroughly to restore the original shape.

distance from the neckline edge down to that point.

Use the silk floss to outline the edges of the petals, working with short pieces since the floss tends to lose its form. Roll your needle a few times between your thumb and first finger to restore the twist. The outline stitch lies along the edge of each petal, beginning near its base and ending at the tip. Start the outline where the petal begins to widen so the floss doesn't get lost beneath the petal. Bring the needle back out at the tip, catching only a tiny bit of cloth; you want the outline to appear as a continuous edging.

Finally, sew the pearls and seed beads in place using a size 12 beading needle and lightly waxed thread. To anchor the entire embroidery, use cotton thread on the back of the work to tack down all the loose ends of the ribbon and floss, without disturbing the work on top.

Another flower option is to make a rose from twisted silk-ribbon cord. Simply coil a length of twisted cord into a soft spiral, and anchor it to the fabric with invisible hand stitches. Embellish around the flowers with leaves, and sew a few seed beads at the center if desired.

For a hand-embroidered leaf Just a few stitches in 4mm or 7mm silk ribbon can create a delicate leaf. If you're covering the spot where a tie or strap joins a gown, arrange a few stitches to cover the join, sewing in spokes from a central point. Stitch loosely, using a blunt needle to encourage the ribbon into a soft, leaflike shape.

As you can see, it's not quantity but quality that determines success in embellishing lingerie. Take your time. At first, use just a single technique on a garment, then build your skills gradually. Before you know it, you'll find that you've brought your skills up a notch, had fun in the process, and are yearning for more.

RESOURCES

Lingerie Patterns, Fabrics, and Findings

Élan Pattern Co.
534 Sandalwood Dr.
El Cajon, CA 92021
(619) 442-1167
www.elanpatterns.com
Bra patterns including large sizes, fabrics, elastics, findings; brochure $1

Fay's Fashion and Fabrics
1155 Webster Dr.
Pensacola, FL 32505-4553
(850) 455-2410; fax (850) 455-7866
www.faysfabrics.com
Lingerie fabrics, findings, patterns; catalog $5, includes $5 certificate

Joyce's Fabrics
P.O. Box 381
Morrisville, NY 13408-0381
Cotton knits, Lycra blends, lingerie fabrics, patterns, elastics; catalog $2 and LSASE, plus $0.10 for each sample

Kieffer's Lingerie
P.O. Box 719
Jersey City, NJ 07307
(201) 798-2266
www.kieffersfabrics.com
Lingerie fabrics, patterns, lace, elastics, trims; free catalog

Kwik-Sew Pattern Co.
3000 Washington Ave. N.
Minneapolis, MN 55411-1699
(888) 594-5739
www.kwiksew.com
Wide range of patterns including lingerie, bras; catalog $5

Laceland
P.O. Box 1504
Sugarland, TX 77487-1504
(281) 983-5223
www.laceland.com
Lingerie fabrics, patterns, laces, findings; catalog $3 plus samples $2

Logan Kits
686 County Rd., 3053
Double Springs, AL 35553
(205) 486-7732; fax (205) 486-0070
www.logankits.com
Lingerie fabrics, patterns, kits, findings; brochure $1.50

Bra-makers Supply
480 Hood Rd., Unit 5
Markham, ON L3R 9Z3, Canada
(905) 948-1396
www.bramakers.com
Lingerie fabrics, patterns, lace, findings; free catalog

Sew Sassy Lingerie
810 Wellman Ave., NE
Huntsville, AL 35801
(256) 536-4405, (800) 67-sassy
www.sewsassy.com
Lingerie fabrics, patterns, laces, findings; catalog $2

Stretch & Sew
P.O. Box 25306
Tempe, AZ 85285-5306
(800) 547-7717; fax (480) 966-1914
www.stretch-and-sew.com
Lingerie patterns including sports bras, elastic, notions; catalog $1

General Fabrics

B & J Fabrics
263 W. 40th St.
New York, NY 10018
(212) 354-8150
Designer fabrics; free swatches

Banksville Designer Fabrics
115 New Canaan Ave.
Norwalk, CT 06850
(203) 846-1333
Designer offcuts at great prices; $10 (refundable) for 36 swatches

Josephine's Dry Goods
521 SW 11th Ave.
Portland, OR 97205
(503) 224-4202
Beautiful silks, cotton knits, laces; swatches $3

Mulberry Silks & Fine Fabrics
Historic Carr Mill Mall
200 N. Greensboro St.
Carrboro, NC 27510
(919) 942-7455
Beautiful selection of fabrics

Paron Fabrics
56 W. 57th St.
New York, NY 10019
(212) 247-6451
Designer offcuts; free swatches; 2 other store locations

The Rain Shed
707 NW 11th St.
Corvallis, OR 97330
(541) 753-8900; fax (541) 757-1887
Cotton knit and ribbings, Lycra blends, Polartec, patterns, notions; catalog $1; swatches available

Satin Moon Fabrics
32 Clement St.
San Francisco, CA 94118
(415) 668-1623
Beautiful, unusual fabrics; swatches $5

Stonemountain & Daughter
2518 Shattuck Ave.
Berkeley, CA 94704
(510) 845-6106
www.stonemountainfabric.com
Wide variety of fabrics; swatches $5 (up to 20), refundable

Threadwear and Sewing Workshop Collection
1250 SW Oakley Ave.
Topeka, KS 66604
(800) 466-1599
www.sewingworkshop.com
Wide variety of fabrics; Japanese-inspired patterns

Beads, Snaps, Silk Ribbon, Dyes, Pattern Paper
Beadworks
149 Water St.
Norwalk, CT 06854
(800) 232-3761
www.beadworks.com
Beads, findings; catalog

The Bee Lee Co.
P.O. Box 36108
Dallas, TX 75235-1108
(800) 527-5271
Western sewing supplies, large selection of pearl and metal snaps, attaching tools, trims; free catalog

Capitol Imports
P.O. Box 13002
Tallahassee, FL 32317
(800) 521-7647
Imported laces, fabrics, ribbon (wholesaler only, but they will provide information about retailers around the U.S.)

Dharma Trading Co.
P.O. Box 150916
San Rafael, CA 94915
(800) 542-5227
www.dharmatrading.com
Fantastic selection of dyes including Jacquard, textile paints, supplies, fabrics, silk ribbon; very helpful free catalog

Elsie's Exquisiques
7225 Lenox Ave.
Riverside, CA 92504
(800) 742-7455, (909) 780-3737
Reproduction and antique trims, laces, silk roses, fringe, ribbon

General Bead
317 National City Blvd.
National City, CA 91950
(619) 336-0100
www.genbead.com
Gorgeous beads, including size 15 Japanese seed beads; catalog $4

Knight's Thread Express
75 McIntire Rd.
New Gloucester, ME 04260
(888) 826-1519
www.threadexpress.com
Silk ribbon and hand-embroidery threads including Kreinik Soie Ping Ling, six-ply filament silk

Screen Process Supplies Mfg.
530 MacDonald Ave.
Richmond, CA 94801
(510) 235-8330
Inkodye in 14 colors and clear

Sew/Fit Co.
5310 W. 66th St.
Bedford Park, IL 60638
(708) 458-5600, (800) 547-4739
fax (708) 458-5665
www.sewfit.com
Sewing supplies, cutting mats, books, videos

The Sewing Place
P.O. Box 111446
Campbell, CA 94011
(800) 587-3937; fax (408) 252-8445
www.thesewingplace.com
Fabrics, patterns, Mönster sewable pattern paper, Wiggle Weights, Fix Velour soft hook-and-loop tape

The Snap Source
P.O. Box 99733
Troy, MI 48099-9733
(800) 725-4600
www.snapsource.com
Wide range of snap sizes and colors, affordable attaching tools; free catalog

SouthStar Supply Co.
P.O. Box 90147
Nashville, TN 37209
(615) 353-7000
www.southstarsupply.com
Pattern paper by the 200-ft. roll, 48 in. wide, item #MP6-48, supplies, notions, and accessories; free catalog

Universal Synergistics
P.O. Box 2840
Wilsonville, OR 97070-2840
(503) 625-2323; fax (503) 625-4329
www.beadcats.com
Beads, books; catalog $2

Web of Thread
1410 Broadway
Paducah, KY 42001
(800) 955-8185; fax (270) 575-0904
www.webofthread.com
Silk ribbon, embroidery supplies; catalog $3

INDEX